from Mother *to* Daughter

from *Mother* to Daughter

Traditional housekeeping for the modern home

Vivienne Bolton

Photographs by Catherine Gratwicke

First published in Great Britain in 2009 by
Kyle Cathie Limited
122 Arlington Road
London, NW1 7HP
www.kylecathie.com

ISBN: 978 1 85626 882 0

A CIP catalogue record for this title is available from the
British Library

10 9 8 7 6 5 4 3 2 1

Vivienne Bolton is hereby identified as the author of this
work in accordance with section 77 of Copyright, Designs
and Patents Act 1988.

Design: Isobel Gillan
Photography: Catherine Gratwicke
Stylist: Ali Allen
Editor: Judith Hannam
Copy editor: Angela Koo
Production: Gemma John

Colour reproduction by Scanhouse in Malaysia
Printed and bound in China by C&C Offset

Acknowledgements
I'd like to acknowledge the inspiration, affection and
friendship I have received from so many strong women
through my life, in particular my grandmother Ella Waters
and my aunts Heather, Dorothy, Sheila and June, cousins
Marcia, Peta, Gail and Jackie, my school-friends Daphne and
Carole, my woman's group, Gayle Wade, my daughters
Zolii, Bianca, Sophie and Chloe, sister-in-law Ruth, my sister
Patricia and Pearl, Jess, Sophie my agent at MBA, and the
crowd of kids now men and women who have down the
years cooked in my kitchen and sat around my table eating
and talking and drinking and laughing and brought joy to
my life, to name just a few of them: Beth, Izzy, Molly,
Naomi, Eva, Becky, Jack, Sim, Corin the list goes on…
oh, and Graham and Hugh and PJ Judges for giving me his
mother's, Jessie's, recipe for pasties.

Thanks to Kyle Cathie for making this book possible and
Judith Hannam for her thoughtfulness, patience and
enthusiasm for this project.

Important note to readers
This book contains information on herbs and remedies
that can be used medicinally. It is not, however, intended
as a medical reference book. Before trying any remedies,
herbal or otherwise, the reader is recommended to
sample a small quantity first to establish if there is any
adverse or allergic reaction. The reader is also advised
not to attempt self-treatment for serious or long-term
problems without consulting a qualified doctor. Neither
the author or the publisher can be held responsible for
any adverse reactions to the recipes, recommendations
or instructions contained herein, and the use of any
remedy or herbal derivative is entirely at the reader's
own risk.

Contents

Traditions passed from mother to daughter

I was born in January, the eldest of six, the first of a new generation. My father was English, my mother a South African, descended from French Huguenots, women with black eyes, and thick dark hair, once farmers, who made their homes in the fertile river valleys of the Cape of Good Hope.

We enjoyed an Enid-Blyton style childhood in the sub-tropical paradise of South Africa, spending many hot afternoons with our Xhosa nannies, walking along disappearing paths through the bush, searching to find and appease a local tokoloshe, now and then reaching down to pick 'vinegar' leaves to chew, much as my children would snack on sweet cicely seeds in our English garden.

In Africa it is traditional for the first grandchild to spend a lot of time with her grandmother. Mine lived old-style, a careful housekeeper, wasting nothing. To earn a living she was a dressmaker, working from home with time to spare she nurtured a sub-tropical vegetable garden and orchard. In the lushness I recall patches of pineapples, mango and lemon trees, beds of fat, oddly-shaped red and orange tomatoes and trailing pumpkin and sweet potato plants. Through the seasons my grandmother taught me: we baked bread and made jams and jellies and preserves. She showed me how to magic up handcream from melted beeswax and scented almond oil, and to mash yellow soap and sugar into a poultice to draw a splinter. She grew mint outside the kitchen window to discourage flies and was known to sprinkle lavender water on a fresh white hanky and hold it close to ease an occasional throbbing head.

The years rolled by and in 1979 I travelled from the tip of Southern Africa to the county town of Bury St Edmunds in Suffolk. I arrived with three little children and a sewing machine. I rented a tumbledown gardener's cottage and invested in half a dozen chickens and some tomato plants. It was spring and the lanes were lined with golden daffodils. In no particular order I settled the older children in the village school, bought copies of Richard Mabey's *Food for Free*, *Wild Food* by Roger Phillips, *Larkrise to Candleford* and John Seymour's *Self-Sufficiency* and dug the vegetable garden.

I have long since grown from that young South African girl and taken on English country ways. In that time I've nurtured gardens, cooked up wonderful jams and jellies, made delicious soft cheeses and one year grew enough carrots to feed a community. I've done much since the children grew up. I've cooked professionally, driven from Canada to Mexico, spent a summer in New York and another in France, made many pots of beeswax and cooked in lots of kitchens. Like my mother and grandmother I am fortunate in having been born with a natural curiosity and a love of knowledge. Nowadays I read and write and paint and cook, and when in the autumn I hear the geese flying over my house calling their return I know I have achieved a certain contentment. This spring I will plant a new garden.

What follows is a journal packed with recipes, home economies, fact and fancies, my book of good housekeeping.

SPRING

My childhood, spent on a sub-tropical beach, meant a steady stream of warm sunny days: spring, summer, autumn and winter pretty much rolled into one. Only high tides and sea horses kept us off the beaches, where acres of golden sand and rock pools full of anemones were the norm. I spent my first spring in Suffolk, a spring full of golden daffodils, leverets, freshly laid eggs and thick Jersey cream – the stuff of storybooks.

A PROMISE OF SPRING

Transplant clumps of early-flowering miniature narcissi or bright blue grape hyacinths into pretty china cups and bowls, place in bedrooms and in little groups on the mantelpiece or windowsill. In the warmth of your home, blossoms will quickly open to fill the air with a subtle fragrance and the promise of spring. For a more heady perfume, pots or bunches of hyacinths will fit the bill. Bulbs need to be set in autumn for spring flowering but cut flowers or near-flowering potted plants can be purchased in spring and carefully transplanted into pretty flowerpots, and you will have a beautiful and economical natural room freshener which will fill your home with head floral scents.

Pretty posies

Bunches of primroses, auriculas, violets, spring leaves and herbs placed in little vases or fish paste jars make pretty bedroom posies.

Informal floral arrangements, freshly picked from the garden and simply placed in jugs or even pretty jam jars will bring a naturalness to your home. If your flowers come from a florist or a market stall, follow life's rhythm and keep them seasonal. Great big bunches of pussy willow or winter jasmine are simple and easily harvested or found for sale at markets. They bring a little spring drama to a room, and branches of willow placed in deep water will quickly sprout green leaves and provide a perfect backdrop to a display of the painted eggs or cotton chicks children love crafting at Easter time.

Daffodils and narcissi

Pick or buy daffodils when their heads are at right angles to the stems, not before. This will ensure that the blossoms open. Once indoors, cut a centimetre from the base of the stems before setting in cool water. If you wish to place these flowers in mixed arrangements with other flowers, trim to length then set alone in water for 24 hours, then transfer to your chosen arrangement. You should not re-cut the stems. Daffodils and narcissi exude a sap that is toxic to other flowers.

Tulips

A bunch of jolly red tulips will brighten up a grey spring day. Pick or buy flowers in bud with a little colour showing. If vase water is changed daily, tulips should have a vase life of a week. Once indoors, cut a centimetre from the base of the stems and set in cold water. My daughter Sophie drops pennies into the tulip water to keep the blossoms proud. When arranging tulips bear in mind that these flowers will continue to grow, moving their head to face the light.

Ranunculus

Once you have your ranunculus blossom home, strip the leaves and trim a centimetre from the base of the stems before placing in water. The stems of ranunculus are particularly delicate so place in a tall narrow vase to keep upright. Change the water daily and set the vase away from fruit and excess heat. Much romantic mythology surrounds these sumptuously delicate blossoms – wonderous stories of eastern princes and frogs and songs of undeclared love. This is one of my favourite flowers.

Lily of the valley

My grandmother's favourite flowers, these bridal blossoms, sweetly perfumed and delicate in appearance, are said to bring happiness to your home. Easy to grow and a joy to find flowering in the garden, plant in a shady spot, harvest flowers and place immediately in water for best effect. Place in a small vase out of sunlight and away from the heat for a long lasting blossom.

Crystallising flowers

Crystallised violets, rose petals, primroses or sweet pea flowers, to name but a few, and some leaves (I like to crystallise mint and lemon balm leaves) can be used to decorate iced cupcakes and other fancies or to pretty-up desserts.

Flower heads or petals should be dipped or painted in either a mixture of gum arabic and rose water or dipped in frothy egg white and sprinkled with caster sugar.

If you would like a very crisp crystallised flower you should repeat the dipping and sprinkling process a couple of times. When crystallising whole flower heads it is advisable to use them immediately as the dip and sugar might not have entered every crevice and therefore the preserving qualities of the sugar might not be sufficient to keep the crystallised flower head for too long.

Gum arabic dip

Measure 50g edible gum arabic into a small bowl, add 4 tablespoons rose water and leave to stand overnight. The following day the gum arabic will have melted into the rose water. Dip the flower heads or petals into the solution then sprinkle with caster sugar. Place on a clean surface to set.

Egg white dip

Place an egg white in a bowl, add a pinch of salt and whisk to a soft froth. Dip flower heads or petals into the froth, then sprinkle with caster sugar and place on a clean surface to set.

Violet-scented perfume

Place a tablespoon of ground orris root in 2 tablespoons of vodka. Set aside in a corked container for 7 days. Strain the liquid through a clean hanky into a small bottle and mysteriously you will have created a violet-scented perfume.

Violets

The intense fragrance of sweet violets conjures up the magic of a bygone age. Wear a posy of sweet violets on your collar to mark the arrival of spring.

Chocolate and Violet Fondant Creams

Makes 450g chocolates

1 egg white
500g icing sugar
¼ teaspoon lemon juice or cream of tartar
essence of violets
violet food colouring
400g good dark chocolate
sugared violets, to decorate the finished chocolates

1 Whisk the egg white lightly with the tiniest pinch of salt and a ¼ teaspoon cream of tartar or lemon juice. Sieve in half the icing sugar and mix well.

2 Add a few drops of essence of violets and colour to a pale violet shade.

3 Knead into a firm paste and roll out onto a clean work surface dusted with a little sifted icing sugar. Roll out to a suitable thickness and use a small round cutter to shape discs. Set aside to dry a little.

4 In the meantime, melt the chocolate in a bowl set over boiling water. Dip each violet-flavoured fondant cream halfway into the chocolate, set down on a non-stick surface, drop a sugared violet onto the chocolate and leave to set.

5 When set, place on a doily-covered plate and serve.

Raspberry and Violet Jam

The violet fragrance intensifies the flavour of raspberry jam, creating an utterly delicious taste. Enjoy with yogurt or on freshly baked scones served with cream.

Makes 1 jar

250g caster sugar
250g raspberries
juice of half a lemon
1 drop essence of violets

1 Preheat the oven to 180°C/350°F/gas mark 4.

2 Measure the sugar into an ovenproof bowl and place in the oven for 15 minutes.

3 Place the raspberries and lemon juice in a saucepan and add the warmed sugar.

4 Heat gently, stirring constantly, and bring to a rapid boil. Allow to boil for 3 or 4 minutes then check for set (*see below*).

5 Remove from the heat and add the essence of violets. Pour into prepared jars, seal, label and set aside to cool.

To test for set

You will need a chilled saucer.

Take a clean spoon and place a blob of jam on the saucer, wait a few moments then press with a fingertip to see if a skin is forming across the surface of the blob. If so, set has been reached and the jam is ready to pot; if not, continue boiling for 4 or 5 minutes then try again.

Mother's tip

I have been known to gently heat a little raspberry jam in a small saucepan and stir in a drop or two of essence of violets before transferring it to a pretty bowl to cool and serve with tea and scones.

SPRING FEASTING

The end of winter and the arrival of spring is celebrated with dancing, spring flowers, rich food and often religious services around the world. Long before the Christian churches celebrated Easter, people danced and decorated themselves and their surrounds with spring flowers and blossoming boughs. Young men and women danced around maypoles and 'queens for a day' were chosen. Lamb is the traditional spring roast and the first leafy vegetables were harvested to enjoy along with all else the spring bounty provided.

In Western Europe, lamb is traditionally flavoured with rosemary and garlic; in Eastern Europe fragrant rose petals and exotic spices or pomegranate syrup are used.

Roast Lamb with Rosemary and Garlic

Some say a little lemon juice squeezed over lamb during cooking gives an interesting and delicate flavour.

Cooking times for a leg of lamb in a 200°C/400°F/gas mark 6 oven:
20 minutes per 500g plus 20 minutes for well-done meat
15 minutes per 500g plus 15 minutes for pink meat

> **2 tablespoons olive oil**
> **1 onion, sliced into thick rings**
> **leg of lamb**
> **1 head of garlic, divided into cloves**
> **fresh stalk of rosemary sprigs**

Preheat the oven to 200°C/400°F/gas mark 6.

Measure the oil into a roasting tin. Create a bed of onion rings for the lamb to roast on. Use the point of your knife to make little slits in the lamb and push a slice of garlic clove into some of them and a little sprig of rosemary into the others. Place the remaining garlic cloves on the onion rings. Season the lamb with salt and pepper and set in the oven.

Gravy

Save all vegetable water to use in the gravy, or use 300ml stock.

Remove the onions from the roasting pan and set aside. Place the roasting pan on a hot stove. If there appears to be a few tablespoons of hot fat in the roasting pan well and good, if not, add a little olive oil. Sprinkle with a couple of tablespoons of flour and begin to stir with a wooden spoon, scraping away at the cooked-on bits, adding their flavour to the mix. When the flour appears to be bubbling, slowly pour in some of the vegetable water or stock, allowing it to thicken. Continue to add liquid, mixing constantly to prevent lumps, until you are happy with the thickness of the gravy. Season and then strain the gravy into a hot gravy boat or jug. Alternatively, transfer the gravy to a small saucepan, add the onion rings and bring to the boil. Taste for seasoning.

Serve with roast potatoes and spring greens

Spring greens: sprouting broccoli, young spinach, nettle tops, dandelion leaves, spring cabbage leaves. Chop the leaves roughly and add to a saucepan containing a few centimetres of water and a lump of butter. When the butter has melted, toss in the leaves and put on the lid. Shake and cook for a couple of minutes until the leaves turn a lovely fresh green colour. Serve immediately, seasoned with salt and pepper and a little nutmeg.

Mint Sauce

The balance of flavours in a good mint sauce is very much up to an individual's personal taste! I chop up about half a cup (loosely packed) of mint leaves and put them in a saucepan along with, half a cup malt vinegar, a splash of water, a teaspoon of sugar and a good pinch of salt. Then bring it to the boil and serve. However, some prefer a little more sugar others prefer the vinegar more diluted. Experiment!

To season a new frying pan or wok

This method should be used on pans that do not have a non-stick coating. Wash and dry the pan. Place on a hot stove and add 2 tablespoons sunflower oil (olive oil is also good) and 2 tablespoons salt. Heat until the oil is smoking then remove from the heat. When the pan is sufficiently cooled use kitchen paper or a pad of crumpled newspaper to wipe the pan clean.

If possible it is a good idea to have 4 frying pans: one for frying fish, a second for omelettes, a third for pancakes and a general pan.

My Perfect Pancakes

Shrove Tuesday is pancake day. In the Christian faith this is the day before the start of Lent. Christians would eat up the last of the eggs and sugar, generally emptying the store cupboards of treats in preparation for 40 days of penance, the time of self-denial. Whilst some still follow the faith, others enjoy the coming of spring, celebrating with pancake tossing competitions and tasty treats.

When making pancakes remember: practice makes perfect.

Serves 2

125ml milk
100g plain flour
1 egg
125ml water
2 tablespoons butter

1 Measure the milk into a bowl, add the flour and mix with a whisk until smooth. Add the egg, whisk further, add the water, mix. If at all possible, set aside for 1 hour.

2 Put the butter in a frying pan, place over the heat, then as soon as the butter is frothing and just about melted, pour it into the batter and mix well with a whisk.

3 Replace the pan over the heat. Heat till good and hot, then add just sufficient batter to cover the pan thinly, leave until cooked through, flip with the help of a spatula (or up in the air if you're feeling a little reckless!), cook on the second side, then serve with a sprinkling of cinnamon, a shake of sugar and a squeeze of lemon juice.

Other fillings:

Good dark chocolate, grated

A mixture of Gruyère and Cheddar cheese, grated

Asparagus

Asparagus is actually a seaside plant – it grows through the soft, salty sand, and is still picked wild along coastal areas of North Africa. Of course this wild asparagus is slim and has a stronger flavour than the succulent domesticated varieties. If you are fortunate to have sufficient space you should plant an asparagus bed. It will take a little effort, and a year to wait for your first harvest but once established you will have a supply of asparagus from the first early showings until the plant takes over.

To cook asparagus

Give asparagus a quick rinse in cool water. Hold a single stalk and snap off the woody end. Set a saucepan of water to boil. Asparagus cooks very quickly. Drop stalks into boiling water and boil for 3 or 4 minutes, and they should be ready to eat. If the stalks are a little old they may need a little more cooking. When the edible ends have been cooked toss the woody ends into the water and boil for 7 or 8 minutes. Remove and use the water to make asparagus soup, or as the stock for a hollandaise sauce.

spring

19

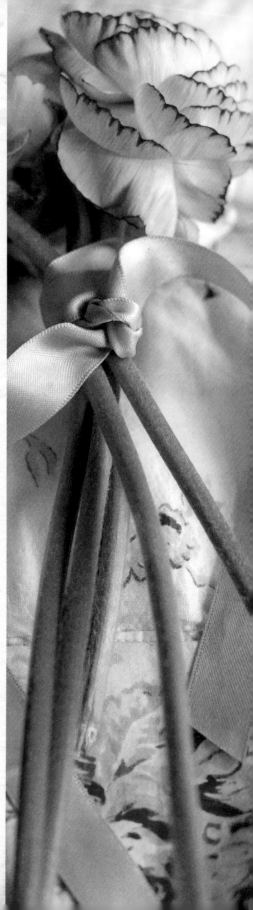

My Simnel Cake

Traditionally, a simnel cake was made by young people in service to take home to their mothers on Mothering Sunday. Nowadays it has become tradition to bake a simnel cake to celebrate Easter Sunday. The rich fruit cake is decorated with 12 marzipan balls for the 12 apostles. My grandmother used to make up this recipe into little fruit cakes, baking the mix in recycled tins, and icing with marzipan and royal icing. They made lovely Easter gifts at a time when good chocolate was difficult to find. Some years I make miniature individual cakes, using this recipe and decorate them with crystallised flowers.

200g plain flour	100g mixed peel
1½ teaspoons baking powder	juice and rind of 1 orange
1½ teaspoon ground mixed spice	50g ground almonds
½ teaspoons ground cinnamon	150g softened butter
300g raisins	150g soft brown sugar
100g currants	3 eggs
100g sultanas	500g marzipan

1   Preheat the oven to 160°C/325°F/gas mark 3. Sift the flour, baking powder and spices into a bowl. Place the dried fruit in a second bowl and add the orange juice. Mix the butter and sugar in a large mixing bowl with a wooden spoon or an electric whisk until light and fluffy. Add the orange rind, ground almonds, and the eggs, one at a time, beating well after each addition.

2   Fold in the flour a few spoonfuls at a time. Fold in the orange juice-soaked fruit – the mix should have a dropping consistency. Butter a 20cm baking tin and line with buttered greaseproof paper. Spoon the mixture into the baking tin. Bake for 2 hours, then reduce the oven to 150°C/300°F/gas mark 2 for 30 minutes.

3   Remove from the oven and leave in the baking tin to cool. When cool, turn out of the tin and onto a plate, then paint the top with warm jam and cover with marzipan. It is traditional to roll 12 small marzipan balls and place around the edge of the marzipan layer, but I prefer to ice over the marzipan with white royal icing and decorate with a posy of crystallised spring flowers.

SPRING HARVEST

An ounce of prevention is worth a pound of cure. Nature's tonic garden: nettles, dandelions, rhubarb, parsley, lemon balm. Tonics refresh the digestion, lift the spirits, boost natural immunity, activate the kidneys and liver and generally promote natural detoxification.

Rhubarb

I discovered rhubarb during my first spring in England. My landlady gave me a carrier bag full of the stuff and I was lost as to what to do with it! She mentioned that the juice and rind of an orange greatly improves its flavour, and so my first rhubarb crumble contained just that. I experimented with the other flavours available at that time of year, hence the Rhubarb and Elderflower Jam, and after eating a jar of rhubarb chutney purchased at the local WI Market, this also became a firm favourite.

Roasting rhubarb

Only the stalks of the rhubarb plant are edible. Leaves should be cut off and discarded, along with 2cm of stalk. Rhubarb should not be cooked in aluminium pans.

The flavour of rhubarb is much intensified by gentle roasting. If you enjoy rhubarb fool be sure to roast the rhubarb sprinkled with a little sugar, mash it when cooked, then add a little more sugar to taste and fold into a half and half mixture of good custard and whipped cream. Serve with a dribble of rhubarb or elderflower cordial for a taste sensation!

Rhubarb and Elderflower Jam

Makes 5 jars

10 elderflower blossom heads
2kg rhubarb
2kg sugar
6 tablespoons fresh lemon juice
grated lemon rind and pips

Place the lemon pips and elderflower blossoms in a loose muslin bag, tie the neck of the bag well and drop into a large saucepan. Wash and chop the rhubarb stems into 2cm lengths and place in a large saucepan. Add the sugar, lemon juice and rind and 150ml cold water. Leave to sit overnight.

The following day bring slowly to the boil, stirring occasionally to melt the sugar. Continue to boil until set is reached (*see p.15*).

Once your jam has reached set, remove the pot from the heat. Wait a couple of minutes to allow the jam to go off the boil then use a ladle to pour into clean prepared jars. Cover and set aside to cool. Label and store.

Rhubarb Chutney

1kg rhubarb
500g onions
500g sultanas
500g soft brown sugar
juice of 2 lemons and a few curly slices of
    lemon rind
½ teaspoon peppercorns
½ teaspoon coriander seeds
2 teaspoons garam masala
3 garlic cloves
20g salt
3cm piece fresh ginger
a few cardamom seeds
250ml white wine vinegar

Chop the rhubarb into centimetre-long chunks and place in a large saucepan. Peel and chop the onions and add to the pan. Add all the remaining ingredients and bring slowly to the boil. Turn down to simmer gently until thick and tasty (about half an hour). Remove from the heat, fish out the ginger and spoon into jars. Label and store.

Rhubarb and Orange Crumble

500g rhubarb
100g sugar
juice and rind of 1 orange
300g plain flour
75g sugar
150g softened butter

Preheat the oven to 180°C/350°F/gas mark 4.

Chop the rhubarb into 2cm chunks and place in a baking dish. Add the sugar and orange rind and juice, toss to mix.

To make the crumble, place the flour in a mixing bowl, add the sugar and softened butter. Use your fingertips to turn the mix into a breadcrumb-like texture. Spoon over the rhubarb and bake for about 40 minutes. Serve with home-made custard (*see p.31*).

Rhubarb Tonic Cordial

This mild natural stimulant renews, bringing vigour and vim.

Take a bunch of freshly picked rhubarb and trim 2cm down from the leaf end and 2cm up from the base. Chop the stalks into 2cm chunks and place in an enamel or stainless steel saucepan. Cover with water and simmer until soft enough to push through a hair sieve (nowadays a metal or plastic sieve will do!).

For each cup of juice add a cup of sugar and a cup of water. Measure all into a clean saucepan and bring to the boil, stirring constantly. When boiling point has been reached, allow to boil for 2 minutes then pour into bottles and cork tightly.

Take a large spoonful daily through spring or pour a little into a glass and add sparkling water for a traditional spring tonic spritzer.

Wild harvest

Wild garlic or ransoms – use as garlic. The leaves, stalks and bulbs are good in spring salads, tossed into a risotto or eaten in an omelette.

Dandelion leaves – eat the leaves in salads or added to soups and stews.

Early chickweed – strip the leaves from the stalks and eat in salads.

Hawthorn leaves – young leaves should be added to a salad.

Ground elder – young leaves are used as a pot herb, added to spring soups and stews in Scandinavia; in Russia and Lithuania young leaves are eaten in salads.

The first hop shoots – can be eaten chopped in salads.

Sweet cicely – leaves are delicious in salads.

Garlic mustard or jack-by-the-hedge – will bring a gentle flavour of garlic to salads and when chopped in mashed potato. Place a few leaves in a salad sandwich.

Red clover leaves – toss with wild mint and eat as a salad.

Dandelions

A potassium-rich diuretic and mild laxative

Dandelion is a potassium-rich herb and a superior natural diuretic – so it succeeds where many other diuretics fail, easing away water retention without affecting potassium levels. Dandelion tea encourages detoxification and stimulates the liver, reduces uric acid from the system and is a general tonic.

For anyone with a history of gallstones, dandelion tea should only be used with professional guidance.

Try telling the time by blowing away the parachute-seeds from a perfect dandelion clock!

Always harvest wild leaves and flowers away from roads where they may be contaminated by exhaust fumes. Inspect plants carefully before harvesting – only harvest leaves and flowers from healthy looking plants. Take only a few leaves or flowers from any particular plant so as not to damage it. Wash the harvest under running water to get rid of little bugs and any dust and dirt.

Dandelion Leaf Tonic Salad

Dandelion leaves are a powerful diuretic which stimulates the liver, so making the leaves ideal for an early spring salad. Gather young leaves and toss them in the lightest olive oil with just a small squeeze of lemon. Serve this tonic salad with soft-boiled eggs and sliced brown bread and butter for a light, health-giving early spring lunch.

Dandelion Tea

Place 2 leaves in a small china jug, cover with boiling water, allow to steep for 4 minutes then pour into a cup and sweeten if needs be.

Nettles

Immune-boosting, anti-inflammatory, de-tox, vitamin-rich

Drinking nettle leaf tea boosts the immune system and promotes the excretion of excess fluids. Nettle tea has become popular in Germany for treating bladder infections and other inflammations of the lower urinary tract. This is because, in addition to promoting the excretion of excess fluids (which helps flush out harmful bacteria), the herb has immune-boosting and anti-inflammatory properties.

Nettle tea can also be taken to assist in the reduction of hay fever symptoms, such as nasal congestion, sneezing and itchy, watery eyes.

Place a teaspoon of dried nettle leaves or a small handful of fresh nettle leaves in boiling water, simmer for a minute or two then pour into a clean cup and sweeten with a little honey if you like.

Nettle Soup

Nettles have traditionally been eaten wherever they have grown. Use nettle tops in soups and added to stews, cooked up with barley and wild garlic. In a good stock they make a tasty and filling meal on a chilly spring day.

> **2 medium onions, chopped**
> **olive oil**
> **2 medium potatoes, peeled and chopped**
> **bunch of nettle tops**
> **500ml vegetable stock**
> **salt and pepper to taste**
> **nutmeg**

1 Fry the onions gently in a little oil until soft, then add the potatoes. Add the nettle tops, toss all together.

2 Pour over the stock and bring to the boil, then simmer until the potatoes are soft.

3 Blend until smooth, add salt and pepper to taste and grate in a little nutmeg. Bring to the boil once more and serve.

Nettle Beer

Makes 12 bottles

½ bucket nettle stalks
12 litres boiling water
1.5kg sugar
50g cream of tartar
15g yeast

Give the nettles a quick rinse, then place them in a large saucepan with water and bring to the boil. Turn down the heat and simmer for 15 minutes. Strain the nettle liquor off into a large container. Measure the strained off liquor and make up to 12 litres with boiling water. Add the sugar and cream of tartar, stir well to mix. Set aside until it cools to body temperature. Add the yeast, stir well and cover with a clean cloth. Leave for 3 days.

Your nettle beer is now ready to bottle. This is best done by siphoning the liquid from the bottom of the container, thus not disturbing the scum and froth floating on top of the beer. Place the container on a table or low stool. Push a plastic tube deep into the beer and suck at the other end of the tube; as soon as the liquid begins to move, push the tube into the first bottle and fill. Put your thumb over the opening of the tube to hold the liquid in place between bottles.

Cork the bottles and set aside for at least a couple of weeks before opening. Nettle beer should be fizzy and fresh tasting and served with ice and a slice!

Elderflowers

The elder tree produces both a spring and an autumn harvest. In the spring the fragrant blossom can be used to flavour drinks, jams and jellies, and can also be used to make creams and ointments. Dipped into tempura batter, whole flower heads can be turned into fragrant fritters to be sprinkled with caster sugar and enjoyed as a spring dessert. Finally, the yeasty blossoms can be used to create the most delicious of fizzy springtime lemonades.

For full flavour and fragrance, always harvest blossoms on a bright, sunny day when the pollen is quite dry and in full flow. The fragrance and flavour comes as much from the pollen, so take care not to shake it, or wash it away. Look over the blossoms well, pick off any bugs and use. Oh, and it is said that every elder tree has a resident witch, so be sure to ask permission from the witch before harvesting begins!

Elderflower Ointment

Rest a bowl over a saucepan of simmering water, add 125g petroleum jelly and 4 cups elderflowers (without the thick stems). The petroleum jelly will melt and in the heat the fragrance and healing power of the elderflowers will be absorbed. Allow to sit over the gently simmering water for 30 minutes. Remove from the heat and immediately strain through muslin into small pots.

Useful in the treatment of chapped hands and for greasing cows' udders and teats.

Elderflower Refreshing Skin Lotion

Place 2 cups of elderflower blossoms in a china bowl. Cover with 500ml boiling water. Set aside for an hour then strain through muslin to make elderflower water. Discard the flowers, add 125ml witch-hazel and bottle the liquid. Use as a refreshing lotion on the face. Store in the refrigerator for up to 4 weeks.

Elderflower Fizz

The pollen of elderflowers contains just enough yeast to give this fragrant lemonade a fizz. Harvest the blossoms on a bright sunny day when the pollen is dry and the bees are buzzing.

700g unbleached white sugar
20 elderflower blossom heads
2 tablespoons wine vinegar
juice and peeled rind of 1 lemon

Pour 4.5 litres of fresh water into a large container, along with the sugar. Stir until the sugar has dissolved. Add the blossoms, vinegar, lemon rind and juice to the solution. Cover with a clean tea towel and set aside for 24 hours.

Strain the liquid into a clean jug and pour into clean screw-top bottles. Set aside in a cool spot for 3 weeks. Open and check for flavour and fizz. If all has gone to plan you should have a fragrant fizzy drink. Elderflower Fizz is best refrigerated.

Muscatel Fruit Syrup

1kg gooseberries
1kg sugar
250ml water
6 elderflower blossom heads

Place all the ingredients in a large saucepan. Bring slowly to the boil. Reduce the heat to a simmer and cook gently for a further 5 minutes. Strain through muslin and bottle. This syrup should be stored in the fridge. To use, mix with sparkling water for a drink fragrant with gooseberries and elderflowers.

Elderflower Cordial

1 litre water
1.5kg unbleached granulated sugar
20 elderflower blossom heads
75g citric acid
juice and peel of 2 unwaxed lemons

Measure the water into a saucepan and add the sugar, bring slowly to the boil, stirring constantly until the sugar has dissolved. Remove from the heat. Add the elderflowers, citric acid, lemon juice and peel. Set aside for 24 hours. Return to the stove, bring to the boil, then remove from the heat. Strain through muslin into a jug and pour into bottles. Seal and store in the fridge.

Enjoy poured over lemon ice cream or added to fizzy or still mineral water with ice and a slice.

EGGS – NATURE'S CONVENIENCE FOOD!

You can't make an omelette without breaking eggs.

Buy free-range eggs as fresh as possible. Never store eggs in the fridge – buy as many as you expect to eat over a few days and store them at room temperature in a basket. All recipes require that eggs should be at room temperature. Mayonnaise will not mayo if the egg yolks are too cold, boiled eggs will crack and egg whites won't whip up as well as they should! Do not wash eggs, the porous shells have a natural covering which protects them well enough.

How to blow an egg

Wash the egg. Use the point of a fine knitting needle or a darning needle to make a small hole at each end. Push the needle through to break the yolk. Blow through one hole, forcing the liquid egg through the other hole and catch it in a bowl (use for scrambled eggs or in a sponge later that day). Rinse blown eggs through with cold water, dry and they are ready to paint or cover with tissue paper, or simply hang on an Easter display.

Easter eggs

The shells of fresh eggs can be dyed with food colouring – add a little vinegar and salt to the water to encourage the dye to take. Once coloured and cool, scrape away at the colour with a darning or knitting needle to make patterns.

Cultures around the world decorate eggs in springtime, colouring them with dyes, painting them or drawing on them.

Boiled eggs, perfect timing

I have a favourite little saucepan I use for boiling eggs. It is an idea to boil eggs in the same saucepan each time – this way you will learn, through trial and error and following the timings set down below, how to boil an egg to perfection!

Place a maximum of 3 eggs in a small saucepan. Cover the eggs with at least 2.5cm of cold water, add a pinch of salt and place the pan on a high heat. When the water is almost boiling, set a kitchen timer for one of the timings below:

3 minutes: really soft-boiled yolk, set white

4 minutes: slightly set yolk, set white

5 minutes: firmer yolk and white

6 minutes: hard-boiled, slightly soft yolk

7 minutes: firmly hard-boiled

Coddled Eggs

Break fresh eggs into a china egg-coddler, place in gently simmering water and check regularly, until cooked to your satisfaction. Serve with toast.

An ostrich egg can feed a dozen people.

Egg white has been used as glue for thousands of years – try it, it works wonderfully.

Crush up eggshells and sprinkle around plants to discourage slugs and snails.

Add eggshells to vinegar and allow to steep overnight, use the liquid to remove stubborn marks from crystal.

Cover an egg yolk with cold water to keep fresh in the fridge.

A fertilised hen egg takes 21 days to hatch.

Victorian cottagers used to stir sparrow eggs into warm tea as a treat!

How to tell whether an egg is fresh

Fill a glass bowl with cold water. Place the egg in the water. If the egg lies on the bottom it is fresh. If the egg tilts slightly upwards it is a few days old. If the egg floats to the surface it is certainly stale.

Egg stains

Wipe and scrape off as much of the egg as you can, then sponge with cold water. If the stain is still there, make a paste of cream of tartar and water, spread across the stain, leave for 10 minutes then rinse well. Wash as normal.

Smoked Salmon and Scrambled Eggs

Perfect for a late night supper or a romantic breakfast. Serve with hot buttered wholemeal toast.

Serves 2

4 slices smoked salmon
4 large eggs
2 tablespoons single cream or 1 tablespoon cream cheese
freshly chopped parsley
1 lemon, cut into thin wedges
black pepper

Shred two of the smoked salmon slices and save the rest for the garnish. Whisk the eggs in a buttered bowl and place over a saucepan. Use a wooden spatula to stir the eggs continuously. When the mixture begins to set in curds, add the cream and continue cooking until you have a mixture of curds and soft creamy egg. Remove immediately from the heat, toss in the shredded smoked salmon and give a last stir, then serve on warmed plates. Garnish with a sprinkling of chopped parsley, a roughly folded slice of smoked salmon and a wedge of lemon. Add plenty of black pepper and serve immediately.

Egg and Bacon Pie

Traditionally this is made on a dinner plate. I use an old white plate for making plate pies. You could use a 21 cm shallow cake tin. Chop 4 streaky smoked bacon rashers into small pieces, fry gently until cooked. Thinly line a buttered pie plate (or tin) with rough puff pastry. Break 2 eggs into the pastry. Break 2 further eggs into a small bowl, season with salt and pepper, whisk lightly and pour into the pastry. Set the cooked bacon in the egg. Cover with a crust of rough puff pastry, brush with a little beaten egg or milk and set in a hot oven. Bake for 25 minutes at 200°C/400°F/gas mark 6 until golden brown. Good hot or cold.

Real Custard

Custard can be made using custard powder and milk but real custard is made from eggs and milk, flavoured with vanilla and sweetened with caster sugar. The custard can also be enriched by replacing some of the milk with cream. To make a trifle, layer soft fruit, sponge cake dipped in sherry, and real custard (made with an equal quantity of double cream) with whipped double cream folded into it – exceedingly good!

Makes 500ml pouring custard

500ml milk

½ teaspoon vanilla extract

4 egg yolks

30g caster sugar (or to taste)

1 heaped teaspoon cornflour mixed in a little milk or cream

Place all ingredients in the top of a double boiler or in a bowl set over a saucepan of boiling water. (Custard can be made in a saucepan directly over the heat, HOWEVER it sometimes burns!) Stir with a wooden spoon or whisk until the custard is thick enough to coat the back of the spoon. At this stage remove from the heat and serve. If you wish to keep it for some time, cover with a sheet of greaseproof paper across the surface to keep a skin from forming. When required, reheat and then pour into a warmed jug to take to the table.

Chloe's Portuguese Custard Tarts

The Portuguese are renowned for their custard tarts. When my youngest daughter began to cook she took on custard tarts. Over the years she has developed her recipe and in our family it has become a tradition to enjoy freshly baked custard tarts made by Chloe on special occasions. Enjoy for breakfast or as a mid-morning treat – add a cup of good coffee, close your eyes and you will almost smell Portugal in your home!

Makes 12 tarts

3 egg yolks

2 tablespoons cornflour

100g sugar

250ml single cream

125ml milk

2 teaspoons vanilla extract

large piece of lemon rind

250g puff pastry

Preheat the oven to 200°C/400°F/gas mark 6.

Place the egg yolks, cornflour, sugar and cream in a saucepan, whisk well until there are no lumps, add the milk, vanilla and lemon rind. Place over a gentle heat and begin to cook, stirring constantly. The mix should thicken into a fragrantly thick custard. Remove from the heat and set aside.

Roll the block of pastry out to double its size then roll up into a tight cylinder. Use a knife to cut into discs, then a rolling pin and a sprinkling of flour to flatten into shapes that will fit into a buttered muffin tray. Fill each shape two thirds with custard. Bake for 15–20 minutes or until golden brown and risen. Eat while still warm from the oven.

The magic of mayonnaise

My grandmother used a fork to magic up mayonnaise. She would place an egg yolk in a small bowl and armed only with a fork and jug of olive oil she would whisk up mayonnaise. I simply don't have her touch – my mayonnaise making equipment includes a balloon whisk. My friend Annie makes her mayonnaise in the blender. After dropping in a couple of egg yolks, a sprinkling of salt, a pinch of powdered mustard and a little slosh of white wine vinegar, she switches on the blender and in a steady stream pours in the olive oil. In no time at all she has a bowl of mayonnaise.

The trick with home-made mayonnaise is to have all the ingredients at room temperature, the same room temperature. Eggs should be fresh and olive oil not too strongly flavoured.

To make a bowl of fresh mayonnaise

Place a single egg yolk and a sprinkling of salt in a small bowl. Take a whisk and begin to mix, add the tiniest drop of olive oil, continue to mix, add the smallest dribble of oil, and whisk further. You should notice the emulsifying process begin – the egg yolk appears to absorb the oil. Add yet more oil, only a dribble, and so you continue.

There will come a point when you know for sure that the mayonnaise is taking. Once that point is reached, add oil more boldly, continuing to whisk, do not loose momentum, then suddenly you will find you have a bowl of mayonnaise. Squeeze in the juice of half a lemon, whisk and watch the colour change from butter yellow to near white. Finally, taste and season with a little more salt if needs be and a grind of black pepper.

Serve your mayonnaise in a bowl to enjoy with salad, or combined with chopped parsley and stirred through warm quartered boiled potatoes for a salad. Flavour your mayonnaise with a little garlic or a squeeze of tomato purée, a pinch of sugar and a little vinegar to make a Marie Rose sauce for prawns, or finely chopped dill and capers to serve with home-made fish and chips.

Poached Eggs

You should use fresh eggs – old eggs do not poach well.

Half-fill a saucepan with water, bring slowly to the boil, then turn down the heat until the water is barely moving.

Break the egg into a cup and pour gently into the water. The egg should begin to cook as it touches the water. It is not necessary to stir or add vinegar or anything else, simply wait. After a couple of minutes turn the egg over, then when it has been in the water for just 3 or 4 minutes (less for a small egg), lift out and drain in a slotted spoon.

I enjoy poached eggs on a salad with a little hollandaise (*see p.99*) or mayonnaise (*see left*) for lunch or on toast for breakfast or a Sunday evening supper. Poached eggs are also wonderful served on spinach or served with an interesting selection of steamed spring vegetables and new potatoes with a mild lemon sauce.

CHEESE

I learned to make cheese when I lived in Old Hall. Their dairy was well equipped, and the production of low fat farmhouse cheddar was the norm. I made the full fat version and experimented with soft cheeses, which made good use of the rich creamy milk.

Home-made Cheeses

**Use muslin that has been rinsed in boiling water
and wrung out
1 litre whole milk
2 tablespoons fresh lemon juice
1 teaspoon sea salt
freshly ground black pepper**

Slowly bring the milk to the boil, wait a few seconds then turn off the heat. Add the lemon juice and mix well. As soon as the curds form, strain through the muslin. Place the muslin-held curds in a colander and cover with a plate. Weigh down the plate with a small can of beans or something similar to squeeze out all the whey.

Small Curd Cheese

**4 litres whole milk
125ml natural yogurt
125ml cultured buttermilk**

Heat the milk to blood temperature (37°C). Whisk in the yogurt and buttermilk. Keep at this temperature until the milk has set into a yogurt-like substance. Gently heat the mixture further until it separates into curds and whey.

After a couple of hours tip the curds into a bowl, add sea salt to taste (upwards of a teaspoonful) and shape into a flattened ball. Roll in freshly ground black pepper.

Other serving suggestions

Mix prepared cheese with 4 tablespoons of finely chopped mixed spring herbs.

Roll prepared cheese in finely chopped chives.

Roll prepared cheese into walnut-sized balls and place in a jar of olive oil to which a chilli and a few peppercorns have been added.

Roll prepared cheese into walnut-sized balls and roll some in freshly ground black pepper and some in finely chopped fresh herbs.

Home-made Creamy Yogurt Cheese Hearts

2 litres fresh whole milk or Greek yogurt

Line individual heart shaped moulds with muslin and fill to the brim with natural Greek yogurt. Fold the muslin over the yogurt and cover with a piece of card cut to size and a weight (I use a little coffee cup). Set aside to drain overnight (in the fridge will do). To serve, tip the firmed up soft cheese hearts onto individual plates and spoon a little fruit sauce over them along with a few berries. Enjoy.

Oatmeal Crackers

One should never be without oatmeal crackers. My recipe is a little unusual as the dough is made with oatmeal and olive oil and they turn out wonderfully crisp. Roll thinly and choose a 'house style' for your crackers – mine are always square.

125g fine oatmeal
100g medium oatmeal
¼ teaspoon bicarbonate of soda
¼ teaspoon salt
1 tablespoon olive oil
150ml warm water

1   Preheat the oven to 170°C/325°F/gas mark 3.

2   Butter and flour a couple of baking trays. Measure the dry ingredients into a bowl – the fine and medium oatmeal, the bicarbonate of soda and the salt. Stir to mix. Add the olive oil to the warm water, give it a stir then pour it into the dry mix. Stir with the handle of a wooden spoon until the mixture forms a soft dough.

3   Sprinkle a little fine oatmeal on a clean work surface and roll out the dough to about 5mm thick. I use an old square cutter to shape my crackers; you could cut the rolled dough into squares with a knife or use a round biscuit cutter to shape.

4   Place the shaped crackers on a baking tray, prick with a fork and bake for 15–20 minutes. For a crisp result, turn them over halfway through baking.

5   When cooked, remove from the baking trays and cool on a wire rack, then store in a biscuit tin until required. Uncooked, shaped crackers can be frozen for up to 3 months. When required, place frozen dough shapes on a prepared baking tray and bake from frozen.

Preparing and storing cheese

When making your own cheese use freshly washed and dried muslin. Immediately before use rinse in boiling water, then in cold, wring out with clean hands and the muslin is ready to take the curds.

Soak hard cheese in buttermilk to soften.

To keep cheese soft and prevent it from going mouldy, place a sugar lump in the cheese dish.

Never wrap cheese in plastic wrap, rather store wrapped in greaseproof paper and place in a cheese dish in the fridge.

Cheese is best served at room temperature. A brie or camembert should be placed at room temperature and allowed to mature into a soft runny mess before serving.

SPRING CLEANING

Spring cleaning is best done on a fresh, cloud-free sunny day. Fling open the windows, don an apron, if possible gather a willing team of helpers, and set to work. Tackle one room at a time. Strip beds, wash under-blankets and linen, turn mattresses, air duvets and blankets. Wipe all surfaces with a sweet-smelling home-made disinfectant cleaner. Wipe out cupboards, polish floors, clean the silver. Work from room to room clearing out the cobwebs, freshening the air and in the evening, when your home is spick and span, bathe in a beautifully clean candlelit bathroom, dress in your favourite gown and drink a toast to the coming summer.

Keeping house

In our grandmother's day cleaning materials and tools were a simple affair – wooden-handled brooms and brushes and a selection of cloths and mops. Housekeepers used bicarbonate of soda, distilled vinegar, strong soap and elbow grease to clean their houses. There are a few modern cleaning products I wouldn't be without – my rubber gloves are one – but on the whole I find traditional methods best.

Lemon-scented Furniture Oil

This furniture oil is simple to make and a treat to use. Apply sparingly and buff up to a gleaming shine.

250ml olive oil
20 drops lemon essential oil

Pour the olive oil into a clean dry bottle, add the essential oil and shake well. To use, place a little oil on a soft cloth, wipe onto wooden furniture and buff to polish.

Lavender Furniture Cream

50g beeswax
280ml turpentine
½ teaspoon lavender essential oil

Turpentine and wax are highly flammable ingredients – handle with care.

Place the beeswax in a bowl set above a saucepan of simmering water. Watch carefully and slowly the wax will melt. Once melted remove from the heat and whisk in the turpentine and essential oil; as you whisk so the mixture will begin to set. Pour into a suitable jar. Leave to cool. To use, spread a little wax with a cloth and buff up to a good shine.

Window cleaner

For a smear-free finish to clean windows make a solution of 1 part white distilled vinegar to 4 parts water, pour into a spray container and apply with a chamois or crumpled newspaper.

Equipment and materials

Wooden-handled soft bristle brush for polished floors

Wooden-handled firmer bristle brush for carpets and rough floors

Metal dustpan and wooden-handled brush for sweeping up spills and picking up dirt

Floor mop and squeezy bucket

Brush and buffing cloth

Long-handled feather or lambswool duster

Selection of cloths and dusters

Soft 2.5cm paintbrush for dusting difficult corners

Distilled vinegar

Bicarbonate of soda

Borax

Lemons and lemon juice

Buckets and bowls

Soap flakes

Home-made surface disinfectant

Furniture cream

Cleaning wicker furniture and baskets

10g soap flakes
25g sea salt
500ml warm water
soft scrubbing brush

Place all the ingredients in a bowl, mix well. Gently scrub the basket or piece of wicker furniture. Rinse lightly and allow to dry naturally.

Pollen spills

Pollen can stain dreadfully. Lift pollen spills immediately from clothing, upholstery or carpets using sticky tape.

Cleaning grease spots from carpets

Make a solution of 1 part salt to 4 parts methylated spirits and gently dab at the grease spot until the spot is removed.

Cleaning bamboo

Wipe down bamboo with a mild solution of salt and water. The salt will go some way to prevent the bamboo from yellowing. Wipe dry with a soft cloth.

Cleaning artificial flowers

Place a few tablespoons of fine salt in a paper bag. Take one flower at a time and place the flower head down into the bag, scrunch tight around the stem and give a few good shakes. Remove.

Brass and copper

Mix equal parts of salt, white flour and vinegar. Wipe the paste over the item to be cleaned, rinse off in warm soapy water and buff till gleaming.

Kitchen surfaces

Wipe down kitchen surfaces with 1 part distilled vinegar to 6 parts water. Pour the solution into a spray container and have it readily available.

Refrigerators

Empty the fridge once a fortnight. Toss out anything no longer edible. Wash racks and shelves in hot soapy water, and sprinkle bicarbonate of soda on any spills. Rinse and dry with a clean towel. Wipe bottles and jars with a very weak solution of distilled vinegar and water. Place a little bowl containing two or three tablespoons of bicarbonate of soda in the fridge, as this will absorb any food odours.

Wooden chopping boards

Wooden chopping boards are far superior to man-made surfaces. Scrub with a little vinegar or lemon juice and salt to clean and disinfect them.

Wooden kitchen tables

Scrub with a brush and a little vinegar in water to clean. Wipe down with a touch of lemon and Lemon-scented Furniture Oil (*see p.38*).

Cleaning silver

real aluminium foil
500ml boiling water
½ cup bicarbonate of soda
suitable china, glass or
enamel dish

The cleaning action results
from a chemical reaction
between the aluminium foil
and the bicarbonate of soda.
If, for example, you are
cleaning a small item such as
a silver brooch, you won't
need as large a sheet of foil or
as much bicarbonate of soda
as you would for a large item.
The item to be cleaned needs
to be touching the
aluminium foil. Add sufficient
boiling water to cover then
spoon in bicarbonate of soda.
There will be a mild chemical
reaction, with a gentle fizz, so
stand aside from the
container. After a few minutes
remove and wash in clean
water, then buff with a soft
cloth. Badly tarnished items
may need a couple of
soakings in this solution.

Beeswax and Orange Blossom Scented Floor Polish

100g beeswax
25g soap flakes
200ml natural turpentine
neroli essential oil

Place the beeswax in a bowl set above a saucepan of simmering water. When the beeswax has melted add the soap flakes and turpentine and stir well. Remove from the heat, add a few drops of neroli essential oil and continue to stir until the mixture begins to set. Pour into a wide-mouthed jar or tin. Leave to cool.

Kitchen sinks

Wipe daily with a little bicarb and water, then rinse with clean running water. If you like to leave your sink gleaming, a touch of oil on a soft cloth wiped over the sink and metal taps will do the trick.

Limescale away

Clean away limescale with vinegar and bicarbonate of soda. Use an old toothbrush to reach difficult spots. When clean, wipe dry with a soft cloth.

Keep the shine

When you have cleaned all the metal surfaces in your kitchen and the kettle is sparkling and the saucepans shine, give them a wipe with a soft cloth dipped in just the tiniest bit of olive oil to keep them gleaming!

Biscuits tins and food containers

Wash in washing-up liquid, dry, and if strange smells seem to linger, a clean cloth sprinkled with vinegar and left in the sealed container overnight followed by a wash may do the trick.

Cookers and ovens

Wipe down with hot soapy water, use a paste of bicarbonate of soda and water to remove tough stains. Rinse away and dry with a soft cloth.

Rusty kitchen tools

Try rubbing with half a potato dipped into bicarbonate of soda. Rinse and dry, then wipe over with a soft cloth and a little olive oil to discourage further rust from developing.

Kitchen tips

Clean the spout of a teapot by packing with salt and leaving overnight.

Stains can be removed from vacuum flasks and decanters by filling with hot water and some rice and then shaking well.

Rubbing your hands with bicarbonate of soda after peeling onions will remove the smell.

Vinegar added to washing-up water will remove fish smells from china.

Natural fungicide

Measure a teaspoonful of tea tree oil into a litre of water, pour into a spray bottle and spray on surfaces to prevent mildew in the bathroom.

Cleaning grout

Make a paste of bicarbonate of soda and lemon juice and use an old toothbrush to clean away dark marks on grout.

SPRING GARDENING

In spring the garden is coming to life, spend time forking over any bare earth to get rid of any early setting weeds, sow nasturtium seeds in pots and plant out pansy seedlings. If you have space sow some cut-and-come again salad seeds and if not sow the seeds in pots to harvest a daily salad.

Latkes

Peel and grate a couple of large potatoes into a colander, leave to stand for a few minutes. Press down on the potatoes to squeeze out as much liquid as possible. Tip the grated potatoes into a bowl, add a couple of tablespoons of flour and salt and pepper, mix well then put a frying pan over a hot stove, add olive oil to about 5mm depth. When the oil is good and hot fry flattened egg-shaped portions of the mixture until golden brown on both sides. Latkes go well with a fried breakfast but can also be served sprinkled with salt and pepper as a snack or as part of a main meal.

Make a tart with a potato crust

Preheat the oven to 180°C/350°F/gas mark 4.

Grate 3 or 4 potatoes onto a clean tea-towel, leave for a few minutes then pull the ends together and squeeze as much of the potato juice away as you can. Tip into a bowl and add a couple of tablespoons plain flour and a sprinkling of salt and pepper, then mix well.

Butter a pie dish, press the grated potato mixture into it to form a pie crust.

Pour in a mixture of 2 eggs and 300ml milk or cream along with 140g grated cheese.

Bake for 40 minutes, then your potato crust tart is ready to eat.

Gnocchi

Delicious little dumplings made from mashed potato, eggs and flour – a traditional Italian dish. Serve with fresh tomato sauce and grated Parmesan cheese.

1kg potatoes
350g plain flour
1 large or 2 small eggs
splash of olive oil

Peel, cook and mash the potatoes. Add the flour and egg and a splash of olive oil, mix well and season with salt and pepper. Form into small balls or flattish shell shapes the size of a very large pea or small broad bean. Cook a few gnocchi at a time in boiling salted water until they rise to the surface. Keep warm and serve immediately with warm tomato sauce and plenty of Parmesan.

The humble potato

Potatoes thrive in a rich soil so be sure to dig in some muck before you plant. Place seed potatoes (a potato which is sprouting) 40cm apart in rows. Initially you will need to keep the potato bed weeded but pretty soon the potato plants will block out the light, so discouraging weeds. Potatoes are ready to harvest once the plants have flowered, which is sometime in summer. Potato flowers and the small fruit are highly poisonous.

If you do not have much space you can still grow potatoes. Use a hammer and a large nail to make holes in the base of a plastic bucket. Place a few pieces of charcoal at the bottom and half fill with potting compost. Place one potato that has begun to sprout on the compost and continue to fill the bucket with compost. Position the bucket in a spot which is sunny in the mornings and shady in the afternoons. Water regularly and at the end of the summer you will have a crop of potatoes.

spring

45

Seeds for salad gardens

Salad leaf mix – harvest young leaves which will come again.

Salad bowl lettuce – harvest a few leaves from each plant.

Oak leaf lettuce – harvest a couple of leaves from each plant.

Spinach – soak seeds before planting, harvest young leaves for salads and stir fries.

Chives – sow an edging of chive seeds around your salad bed to discourage slugs and snails. Use both the leaves and flowers sprinkled in salads.

Sweet cicely – harvest throughout the spring and summer; chop finely and sprinkle on salads.

Parsley – soak seed in water overnight before planting.

Basil – sprinkle a few seeds directly into the soil or in a pot, cover with a layer of fine soil or compost. Water and wait. Harvest leaves and chop off flowering tops as they appear to encourage new growth.

Chervil – a Tudor salad herb, easy to grow and ready to harvest 8 weeks after sowing; add to salads. Simply sow seed directly into the earth and leave to flower and seed.

Grow your own salad

Very little space is required to grow enough greens to enjoy a salad every day.

Dig over an area about 2 metres square. Enrich the earth by digging in some mushroom compost or well-rotted manure. Draw out a rough plan and purchase seeds. On a sunny day when all signs of frost are over and the moon is waxing sow your seeds. Keep your salad garden well watered and if necessary cover with netting to prevent birds and animals from visiting.

If your salad garden is growing against a wall or trellis, plant mangetout peas at the back, and harvest as they appear to keep them coming.

Plant a pumpkin

Time to sow a pumpkin seed – or a few pumpkin seeds, if you have the room!

Soak pumpkin seeds in water for 1 hour. Fill some small plant pots with potting compost and sow a single seed in each pot, about a centimetre deep. Press the soil down firmly and water. Place the pots on a bright but not sunny windowsill in a warm room and water a little each day. Slowly the seeds will germinate and hopefully turn into sturdy plants. Once all possibility of frost is past, plant in the garden in a sunny spot. Water regularly and you will have some fine pumpkins to harvest at the end of summer.

Grow garlic on a sunny windowsill

Plant 3 garlic cloves in a 15cm pot. Use good potting compost and push well into the soil. Place on a sunny windowsill and remember to water regularly – with a little luck they will grow and in time you will have 3 fat bulbs of garlic.

SUMMER

I never quite believed in summer before I came to England. But here, the summer really does mean roses and lavender, peaches and plums, soaring skylarks, fresh lemonade and famously strawberries and cream. Do find time between jam making and summer fetes for a trip to the seaside – make the most of the fine days creating memories to get you through the long cold winter months.

SUMMER GARDENING

Nobody should be without a garden, be it a window box, a plant on a sunny windowsill or an acre of flowers. Gardening soothes the spirit. In all summers of my adult life I've never not grown something to eat.

Kitchen windowsill herbs

It is possible to buy pots of herbs ready for harvesting from supermarkets, but these herbs are grown for immediate use, not for planting or growing on. If you would like to grow pots of herbs on your kitchen windowsill you are advised to purchase healthy looking plants from a garden centre or plant specialist. Don't forget to buy some potting compost too. Once you have the plants home, re-pot into slightly larger, interesting containers. Water them regularly and give them a settling in period before you begin harvesting any leaves. Parsley, chives and basil can all be grown on a sunny windowsill.

Herby window boxes

Chives, parsley, lemon thyme and rosemary all do well in a window box. Plant the lemon thyme in the front of the box, as it is low growing. The chives will bring summer colour and, if the window box is large enough, you may consider a variegated nasturtium or two to creep amongst the other plants and hang over the sides. Window boxes need plenty of watering and regular feeding – never count rain as water!

How to sow seed

As a general rule, seeds need moisture and a suitably warm temperature. Place larger seeds deeper in the soil than tiny seeds. Almost all seeds germinate better in the dark so be sure seeds are covered with a layer of soil or potting compost – seeds left on top of the soil tend to dry out too quickly to germinate. If you are sowing seed out of doors, prepare the ground by removing weeds and digging the soil over, then rake it smooth. It may be an idea to protect seeds and seedlings from slugs and snails, hungry birds or cats that may find the newly dug soil interesting. Do not let seeds or young plants dry out – water with a fine misty spray in the early mornings and late afternoons.

Sow nasturtiums

Nasturtiums come with green leaves or variegated leaves, while the flowers can be anything from the palest yellow, through orange to almost red. Nasturtiums are incredibly easy to grow and richly rewarding. Plant the seeds in pots or in the garden, water well and in just a few weeks you will be able to harvest peppery flavoured leaves for salads and flowers for garnishes. Then later, the green seed pods can also be pickled to make nasturtium capers.

Pickled Nasturtium Pods

Pick nasturtium seed pods when they are fat and green – sufficient to fill a couple of little jars. Boil up 250ml white wine vinegar to which you have added half a teaspoon of salt and a few peppercorns. When the vinegar comes to the boil, remove from the heat and pour over the nasturtium pods, seal and label. These will be ready to eat after about 3 weeks – use just like capers. They are delicious as a salad garnish, on pizzas or chopped and mixed with cream cheese.

summer

Dealing with slugs and snails

Keep a look out for slugs and snails and remove any you find, releasing them to the wild or eliminating them! Sprinkle crunched-up eggshells or grit around salad beds and any especially tender plants. It is an idea to set a few 'slug pubs' around the garden: dig large empty yogurt pots into the earth, half-fill with beer and wait. The slugs will come to a happy end.

How to set a cutting

20cm plant pot
potting compost
dibber (or stick)
watering can and water

1 Some plants can be propagated easily from seeds; some (such as strawberry plants) put out runners – leafy stalks which send down roots of their own. Many plants can be multiplied by dividing a large plant at the roots into smaller plants (asters, tarragon), and there are some plants that take well from cuttings (rosemary, lavender, willow).

2 Take a cutting when flowering is over. A heel cutting is best – pull a healthy looking branch away from the plant in a downward movement and you will be left with a branch with a small heel at the end.

3 Plant the cuttings directly into the earth, in short rows, or fill the plant pot with compost and plant three or four small cuttings in it. Trim away all but a third of the leaves and make a hole in the soil with a stick or a dibber. Drop the cuttings deep into the holes. Press the soil firmly around each cutting and water well.

4 Check on any progress the cuttings have made and in due course you will see fresh growth. When the plants are well established with good roots, transplant them into position. Water well and let nature takes its course. Not all cuttings take successfully, so set more than you think you will need.

Brown paper pots

I use either newspaper or brown paper, fold a sheet of paper in half, creating a large triangular shape, and then roll into a tube of about 12 cm in diameter (I use an empty baked bean tin to make the shape). Fold up and use a length of string to hold in place. Remove the tin and fill with potting compost.

HOME REMEDIES FROM THE GARDEN

Use a summer harvest of herbs and flowers to cook up creams and ointments to use all year round. Hand creams scented with essential oils, rosemary and lavender for gardeners, lighter fragrances for gentlewomen and ointments that capture the healing powers of calendula.

Gardener's hand care

Protect your hands when gardening by wearing gardening gloves, or if you prefer to feel the earth directly, push your nails into a bar of slightly softened soap, then spread a little petroleum jelly over your hands and wrists. When gardening is over, wash your hands well with soap and a little salt and use a nail brush to remove the soap lodged under your fingernails. Apply hand cream, massaging it into your hands and wrists.

Gardener's Hand Cream

2 tablespoons cocoa butter

2 tablespoons beeswax granules or the equivalent quantity cut from a beeswax candle

4 tablespoons almond oil

2 capsules vitamin E oil

10 drops rosemary oil

10 drops lavender oil

6 drops eucalyptus oil

Place all the ingredients in a china bowl set above a saucepan of boiling water. After a few minutes the cocoa butter and beeswax will begin to melt. Take a whisk and slowly whisk the mixture until all is liquid. Remove from the stove and continue whisking. As the mixture cools the whisking will incorporate some air and you will be left with a light fluffy hand cream.

Soothe minor burns with fresh aloe vera gel

Keep a potted aloe vera plant on the kitchen windowsill. To treat minor burns, hold the affected area under cold water for 5 minutes then spread with fresh aloe vera gel. To get at the fresh gel simply snap off a section of leaf and scoop out the gel, then spread it directly onto unbroken skin.

Calendula Ointment

This recipe is a treasure; I was given it not long after the birth of my first child. That boy will be 40 next year and in the intervening years I have made many, many jars of calendula ointment.

2 cups fresh calendula petals
350ml almond oil
50g beeswax

Place the calendula petals and almond oil in a wide-mouthed jar. Set on a sunny windowsill for 2 weeks. Transfer to a small saucepan and place over a low heat, add the beeswax and slowly bring up the heat. Keep at a low heat for 30 minutes then strain through a pre-warmed sieve into a scrupulously clean jar. Use as needed for minor scrapes or as a hand salve.

Feverfew for migraine

Every day make yourself a sandwich, placing a freshly picked feverfew leaf between the slices of bread. After some months migraines should reduce in number and severity.

Hay fever and honey

Enjoy a daily teaspoon of honey harvested from hives local to your home to relieve hay fever symptoms. This is a long-term project, as you need to take the honey for a whole season before it has any effect, but it has certainly worked for me!

A cocktail for a summer cold

Relieve the symptoms of a summer cold with this amazing cocktail.
  In an electric blender place: half a cup of chilled tomato juice, a little squeeze of lemon juice, a splash of soy, a large clove of garlic, peeled, half an onion, chopped, and a few basil and parsley leaves. Add a little ice and blend. Pour into a cocktail glass and drink immediately.

Chew a little parsley to eliminate bad breath.

Relieve the discomfort from a bee sting by laying a slice of onion over the painful area.

Relieve wasp stings with a squeeze of lemon juice.

THE HOME FLORIST

If you have a garden you can grow flowers. Sow seed, or plant seedlings or cuttings in the spring. If you have room in your vegetable garden you can grow flowers in rows for picking; if not then plant your flower beds with cutting in mind.

Caring for your vases

Once used, wash vases in warm soapy water, give the insides a quick scrub with a little distilled vinegar and bicarbonate soda. Rinse and dry upside down if possible. Remember any watertight container can be used to display flowers, and if a much-loved vase has developed a crack, line it with a waterproof plastic bag and fill that with water. Set vases down away from hot radiators and out of draughts (the blossoms will last longer), and do use a coaster or mat under vases, to save polished surfaces.

Caring for cut flowers

Whether you buy your flowers or grow them, once picked and indoors be sure to place the flowers in water immediately.

Harvest flowers first thing in the morning, before the sun is properly up, for longer lasting blooms.

Don't pick daffodils until the flower is sitting at right angles to the stem.

Just before you arrange the flowers in bowls or vases, snip an extra centimetre from the stalks, cutting at an angle, then plunge immediately into water. Change the water daily or at least refresh with cold water.

Flowers that are flagging can be improved by removing them from the vase, trimming their stalks a couple of centimetres and then plunging them into boiling water for 10 seconds before putting in a vase of fresh water along with a good swig of lemonade or a teaspoon of sugar.

If you must use a flower with a broken stem, push the stem into a drinking straw and arrange as usual.

Drop a few copper coins in a vase of tulips to keep them from falling over, or do as my mother-in-law did and prick tulip stems with a pin a few centimetres from the flower heads to keep them standing tall.

Never mix bulbs with annuals.

Remove any leaves or thorns that will be submerged – leaves are likely to decay rapidly in the water, creating nasty smells.

Spritz your arrangements with cold water occasionally to perk them up.

Never place flowers in full sun, near a radiator or in a draught.

Remove stamens from lilies (the pollen will stain the petals, and possibly your clothes) – don't cut them, rather gently pull the stamens off.

Flowers suitable for cutting

Short-stemmed flowers:

Nasturtiums

Pansies

Forget-me-nots

Sweet peas

Pinks

Red valerian

Medium-stemmed flowers:

Marigolds

Zinnias

Nigella

Clary

Daffodils

Tulips

Lily of the valley

Rambling or climbing roses

Long-stemmed flowers:

Irises

Lilies

Mint

Delphiniums

Larkspurs

Hydrangeas

Remove dust from the leaves of pot plants by wiping them with cotton wool soaked in milk.

summer

57

Roses

What woman can resist a bunch of fragrant red rose – certainly not me! I try to always have roses in my room, fresh in summer, pot pourri in winter.

Rose Petal Jelly

500ml water
500g unbleached white sugar
juice of 1 lemon
2 cups fragrant rose petals
3 teaspoons rose water

Measure the water into a saucepan, add the sugar and lemon juice, place over the heat and bring to the boil, stirring to dissolve the sugar. Toss in the rose petals and boil for 7 minutes then test for set (*see p.15*). Once set has been achieved, remove from the heat, add the rose water, stir rapidly and then pour into jars, cover and seal.

Rose Milk Bath

1 cup oatmeal
1 cup rolled oats
1 cup dried fragrant rose petals
8 drops attar of roses
handful of fresh rose petals

Make simple bags of muslin, fill each bag with 4 tablespoons of the mix, tie with long ribbons and place in a large glass jar. To use, suspend two bags from one of the bath taps. Run a bath to a comfortable temperature, sprinkle with fresh rose petals and your oat-milk bath, is ready to enjoy.

Fragrant Rose Hand Cream

The age-old combination of attar of roses, rich cocoa butter and sweet almond oil produces a hand cream that will soften and feed your hands.

Essential oils are highly potent and their use should be closely supervised. Essential oils should never be applied directly onto skin or eaten!

2 tablespoons cocoa butter
40g beeswax
2 tablespoons rosewater
4 tablespoons almond oil
2 capsules vitamin E oil
8 drops attar of roses

Place the beeswax, cocoa butter, rose water and almond oil in a bowl. Set the bowl over a saucepan of very hot water. The beeswax and cocoa butter should melt and mix with the almond oil.

Taking care, remove the bowl from the saucepan and place on the work surface. Add the vitamin E oil. You will need to snip through the soft shell of the capsule with scissors and squeeze the vitamin E oil out into the mixture. Next add the rose essential oil.

Use a whisk to mix the ingredients well together. Continue to whip the mixture with the whisk until it begins to look like soft whipped cream.

Spoon the made up hand cream into pretty wide-mouthed jars. The hand cream should set further as it cools. When the hand cream is set it is ready to use. Don't forget to label your jars.

Rose petals

Rose petals can be crystallised, candied, made into jams and jellies, added to sugars, tossed into salads and used as a garnish for desserts. In Turkey, fragrant rose petals are used to flavour lamb dishes and rice.

Always use flowers that have been grown in a chemical-free environment. Old rose varieties have the best fragrances.

Rose Petals and Wild Rice

Cook a mixture of wild and basmati rice. Just before serving, toss in a small handful of fragrant red rose petals, place over the heat and steam for a minute. The rice will become fragrant with the rose petals and look simply amazing! Serve with a favourite saucy chicken or lamb dish. (This is one time when, I would consider using a microwave – add fresh, fragrant rose petals to cooked wild and basmati rice, toss and place in the microwave for 20 seconds, then serve.)

summer

59

Lavender

It always amazes me that fragrance of lavender I breathe in is the same fragrance smelt by a history of women that goes back thousands of years. I imagine Roman women settling in Britain two thousand years ago would have brought lavender plants with them.

Growing lavender

Lavender thrives in a sunny, well-drained position. Take heel cuttings from an established plant in summer. To do this find a branch about 15cm long, hold it firmly and pull away from the main stem using a downward movement. The cutting should have a 'heel' where it was attached to the main stem. Plant firmly into damp soil, leaving only 5cm of the cutting above ground. Plant a number of cuttings in a row as inevitably some will not take. It will take 6–8 weeks for the cuttings to establish. Transplant to a sunny, well-drained position. Do not over-water.

Lavender flowers from established plants should be harvested when freshly in flower. Flowering stalks should be cut back in autumn to neaten and encourage the plants to bush.

Harvesting lavender

Harvest flowers in small bud in the morning before the heat of the day. To dry, tie in small bunches and hang in a cool dry spot. Freshly harvested lavender can be used to flavour sugar: place 10 flower heads in a jar containing 500g caster sugar, then set aside for 2 weeks. Lavender sugar can be used to flavour shortbread and other sweet delights. Lavender flowers can also be used to scent pot pourri, as a cut flower in summer posies or simmered in oil and wax to scent home-made furniture polish.

Lavender moth protection for woollens

Place dried lavender flowers in muslin sachets and slip between your woollens to keep them fragrant and repel moths. For the same purpose lavender essential oil can be sprinkled onto cotton wool balls and strategically placed in the linen cupboard. Plant lavender underneath your bedroom window, and on summer days the gentle fragrance will not only scent your room but will also help keep out bugs.

A soothing lavender foot bath

Place a suitable bowl on the floor in front of your favourite chair. Pour hot water into the bowl to a depth that will comfortably cover your feet. Add 3 drops lavender essential oil and half a cup of Epsom salts. Once the water has cooled sufficiently, sit down, lower your feet into the water and lie back and relax.

Lavender Hand Cream

3 lavender flower heads
30ml boiling water
30g beeswax
1 teaspoon emulsifying wax
125ml almond oil
10 drops lavender
   essential oil

Pour the boiling water over the flower heads and set aside until cool, then strain through muslin. Set a china bowl over a saucepan of boiling water and add the infused water, and remaining ingredients. Use a small whisk or a tied bundle of hazel twigs to beat until you have a thick cream. Spoon into a clean jar.

summer

Lavender bottles

Pick long stalks of lavender when it is in full flower. For each bottle you will need 11 stalks and a metre of ribbon. Make a bunch and tie the heads tightly together just below the flower heads. The ribbon should have a short end (about 30cm) and a long end. Hold the flower heads in one hand and draw a stalk down over the head. Weave the long ribbon in and out around the stalks pulling them down one after the other around the bunched flower heads. Work your way in and out travelling round the flower heads until you have completely enclosed them. Wind the ribbon twice around the neck of the lavender bottle, draw the other ribbon end in and tie with a bow.

Lavender Honey

A romantic flavoured honey.

Drop 4 lavender flower heads into a jar of runny honey. Close and set on a sunny windowsill for a couple of weeks. Remove the lavender flowers and your flavoured honey is ready to eat.

Lavender Sugar

Place 500g caster sugar in a large glass jar. Add 4 tablespoons of freshly picked lavender flowers and mix in. Sprinkle 6 drops of lavender essential oil onto a cotton wool ball and place in the jar. Seal the jar and give it a good shake. Set aside for 2 weeks. Open, remove the cotton wool ball and sift out the lavender flowers and you will have 500g lavender sugar.

Lavender Shortbread

This should be baked slowly to give a crisp, melt-in-the-mouth shortbread.

> **200g plain flour**
> **50g ground rice**
> **150g lavender sugar**
> **2 heaped teaspoons fresh lavender flowers**
> **two buttered 18cm cake tins**

1 Preheat the oven to 160°C/325°F/gas mark 3.

2 Use your fingertips to rub together the flour, ground rice and lavender sugar. When the mixture has the appearance of breadcrumbs toss in the fresh lavender flowers.

3 Divide the mixture equally between two buttered 18cm cake tins. Pat the dough firmly into place with the base of a tumbler.

4 Bake for 45 minutes. When cooked, allow to stand for a minute or two then slice. Set aside to cool before removing from the tins.

SUMMER FRUIT AND VEGETABLES

A summer glut of fruit and vegetables offers plenty of opportunity to fill the freezer and line the shelves with all manner of delights. Tomatoes can be bottled, dried into jam or chutney and cooked up in sauces to brighten winter months as a reminder of summer.

Sun-dried Tomatoes

Cut tomatoes in half, scoop out the seeds you can easily get at and sprinkle with the tiniest bit of fine sea salt. Lie upside down on a drying rack for an hour or so then turn over and put out in the sun. If the weather is wonderfully hot it should take two or three days for the tomatoes to dry sufficiently to be bottled in olive oil.

Tomatoes dried in this way will be almost leathery to touch but still chewy. Use sliced and sprinkled on salads or pizza or tossed through spaghetti with a little garlic and chilli.

Oven-dried Tomatoes

Cut tomatoes in half, scoop out the seeds and lay on a baking tray. When the tray is full sprinkle the halved tomatoes with a little sea salt and olive oil. Bake in a warm oven, set to the lowest temperature possible. The tomatoes should take about 4 hours to dry. The flavour of tomatoes is intensified by drying in this way. Use in soups and pasta dishes or tossed in salads.

Green Tomato Jam

Makes 4 jars

1kg green tomatoes
1kg unbleached white sugar
juice of 1 lemon
125ml water

Roughly chop the tomatoes. Place in a china or glass bowl, toss in the sugar and lemon juice, cover and place in the refrigerator overnight. Reserve the empty lemon halves.

The next day, pour the mixture into a saucepan, add 125ml water and the empty lemon halves, and bring to the boil over a low heat. Allow to boil for 10 minutes. Remove from the heat and discard the lemon halves. Set aside until quite cool.

Once again bring the mixture to the boil, continue to boil, checking for set every couple of minutes. When set is achieved (*see p.15*) remove from the heat and bottle.

summer

63

Growing tomatoes

If you were to grow only one fruit or vegetable then grow a tomato plant. Fill a large plant pot with good compost, plant a single tomato seedling in the centre and push a good strong stake (this could be a stick or a garden cane) deep into the soil just beside the plant. Water daily and wait. As the plant grows you should tie it to the sturdy stake. To do this loop a length of string or ribbon around the stem of the tomato plant, then cross the string ends over and loop around the stake, thus creating a figure of eight with the string. Done in this way the plant stem is less likely to become damaged.

From now on you will need to regularly remove any branches growing from the 'elbows' of the plant. You don't want the plant to become too bushy as this discourages flowering and ultimately the arrival of fruit. A freshly picked tomato, eaten within half an hour of picking, is full of the flavour of summer.

Fried Green Tomatoes

Slice green tomatoes and roll in a little polenta or oatmeal. Fry in oil and eat as part of a mixed grill or fried breakfast. Delicious.

The great tomato harvest

Be sure to harvest all tomatoes before the first frost. Place any unripe tomatoes in a dry, dark, frost-free place. An old chest of drawers would be ideal – line the drawers with newspaper before storing the tomatoes, not touching. Check up on them every two or three days and in time they will ripen to perfection.

How to skin a tomato

To skin tomatoes, dip in a saucepan of boiling water for 30 seconds, remove and make a nick in the skin, which should then come away readily.

When frying tomatoes sprinkle with a pinch of caster sugar to bring out the flavour.

To ripen green tomatoes, place them in a brown paper bag along with a ripe apple. They should ripen up within a few days.

Tomato Ketchup

Makes 2 litres

4 onions, chopped
4 garlic cloves
olive oil
1 head of celery, washed and chopped
500g carrots, grated
3kg ripe tomatoes
125g unbleached white sugar
250ml cider vinegar
few sprigs of oregano
small bunch of parsley
3 level teaspoons sea salt
good pinch of cayenne pepper
few grinds of black pepper

Fry the onions and garlic in olive oil and when quite soft, add the chopped celery and the grated carrots, turn down the heat and simmer gently for 10 minutes.

In the meantime, skin the tomatoes and chop them into quarters. Add them to the saucepan.

Simmer for a few minutes, then add the remaining ingredients and simmer for 30 minutes.

Remove from the heat, mash well and push through a sieve (or simply put the slightly cooled mixture in the blender until smooth!). Add a little water if you feel the mixture is a bit too thick.

Return to the heat, bring to the boil, then pour it into wide-necked bottles and seal. Store in the fridge.

Fresh Tomato Sauce for the Freezer

The trick with this is to cook a sufficient quantity to freeze in suitably sized portions. When required, use as a base for pasta meals or add to cooked cannellini beans and a little stock for a delicious soup. To make 2 litres of sauce, which could be divided into 4 freezer portions, you will need 3kg ripe tomatoes, a good slosh of olive oil, 250ml water, a sprig or two of oregano, salt and pepper to taste and a couple of teaspoons of sugar – oh, and a glass of red wine if you happen to have an open bottle.

Place all the ingredients in a large heavy-bottomed saucepan and simmer gently for an hour, check on it regularly and fish out the tomato skins as they come away and float to the top. Cool, portion up and freeze for future use.

Fresh Tomato Soup

Serves 4

1.5kg tomatoes
6 shallots
olive oil
3 garlic cloves, chopped
3 celery sticks, chopped
1 tablespoon cider vinegar
pinch of saffron
level teaspoon of sugar
tiny pinch of chilli flakes
200ml water
salt and pepper

Skin the tomatoes and chop them coarsely.

Peel and chop the shallots. Place a large saucepan on a medium heat and add a little olive oil. When the oil has heated add the prepared shallots. Cook gently until opaque then add the chopped garlic and finally the celery. Allow to cook gently with the lid on for 5 minutes.

Add the tomatoes, vinegar, saffron, sugar, chilli and water and simmer gently for 30 minutes.

Remove from the heat and blend. You may need to add a little more liquid. Season with salt and black pepper. Return to the saucepan and heat before serving either simply with sliced wholemeal bread and butter or ...

with a large garnish of cooked prawns and crusty French bread

with a bowl of crisp croutons and garnished with chopped parsley

with a side dish of wholemeal toast and cheese

sprinkled with Gruyère cheese and served with hot crispy rolls

Cherry Brandy

If possible use dark morello cherries. Wash and dry enough cherries to almost fill a bottle, adding a tablespoon of granulated sugar for every 250g cherries. If you have them handy, add a few peeled almonds. Fill the bottle with brandy and seal. Set in a quiet dark spot. Every day for 2 weeks give the bottle a bit of a shake then set aside for 6 weeks when the brandy and fruit will be quite delicious drunk as a liqueur or used to garnish and flavour a special dessert.

How to make jam

The fruit needs to be washed, peeled if necessary, chopped and simmered in just enough water to cover it. Once cooked use a teacup to measure the quantity of cooked fruit in its juice. Return the cooked fruit and juice to the saucepan and add an equal measure of sugar. Bring to the boil, stirring constantly to dissolve the sugar. Boil and watch. At first the bubbles will be noisy and random – some big, some small – and the mixture will bubble up the sides of the pot. Slowly the pattern will change until the bubbles are a sort of blub, blub, blub. Now you need to get hold of a cold saucer and place a teaspoonful of the jammy mixture on it. Wait a minute or so then press down on it with your fingertip. If a skin has formed, the jam has reached set and it is ready to be poured into jars.

The one item I would suggest investing in is a jam funnel. This is placed over the jar and the hot jam is ladled in without spilling down the sides of the jars. Once full, cover the jam with a disc of greaseproof paper and put on the lid. If possible choose jars with good lids, if not buy cellophane discs with elastic bands and use those.

Some fruits are naturally high in pectin and set easily; others contain little pectin and need some help. Apples and crab apples, gooseberries, blackcurrants, oranges, lemons, grapefruit, plums, quinces and medlars all set easily. However, strawberries, raspberries, brambles or blackberries and pears all need a little lemon juice.
Always use cane sugar to make jam as it sets better. The sugar both sweetens and preserves the jam, so be sure to add the suggested quantities.

Sliced Peach Jam

My grandmother made the best sliced peach jam. The syrup just runny enough and the slices of peach never turned mushy.

Makes 6 jars
2kg yellow peaches
granulated sugar
juice of 1 lemon

Place the peaches in boiling water for 30 seconds, then peel away their skins. Slice and discard the stones. Place in a saucepan, cover with water and bring to the boil. Simmer for 3 minutes. Remove from the heat and drain off the liquid. Measure the liquid and return it to the saucepan, adding an equal quantity of sugar. Bring to the boil, stirring constantly to melt the sugar. Add the lemon juice and peach slices and boil until the peaches are cooked and the syrup is thick. Pour into jars, cover and seal.

Granny's Granadilla (Passionfruit) Fridge Cake

This is without doubt a generation of grandchildren's favourite summer pudding. It is simple, modern, and a handy store-cupboard dessert, as it is possible to make it perfectly from tinned and packaged goods!

1 packet lemon jelly
410g tin evaporated milk chilled overnight in the refrigerator
12 granadillas or a good cup of canned passionfruit pulp
1 packet Nice biscuits or South African Tennis biscuits

Make up the lemon jelly with slightly less water than usual. Leave to cool and begin to set. Open the chilled evaporated milk and pour into a large bowl, whip with a hand or electric whisk until it peaks, as fresh cream would, then whisk in the chilled lemon jelly. Fold in the passionfruit pulp. Finally layer up the biscuit and jelly mix in a dish, sprinkling a little crushed biscuit on top. Place in the fridge to set.

Bananas

Remember to use only organic pesticide-free banana skins!

Use organic banana peel laid yellow-side out against the skin on your face as a face mask to reduce wrinkles.

Eliminate warts by taping a square of banana skin, yellow side out over the wart. Change the banana skin dressing daily until the wart goes away.

Fried bananas are a great addition to a breakfast fry-up. Peel, slice into long halves and fry in butter or olive oil.

Wash and chop banana skins. Fry a chopped onion with a little chopped garlic, chilli and ginger. Add the banana skins and a little water. Simmer gently until tender. Add garam masala and season to taste. Enjoy with rice and a little yogurt.

Bananas can be barbequed whole as a dessert; when cooked, open and tip into a bowl, then sprinkle with cinnamon and sugar and a little cream.

Bananas contain serotonin that can help alleviate the symptoms of depression.

SUMMER DRINKS

We must not forget that water is the best summer drink – simple, refreshing, either sparkling or still. If flavouring is required a cordial is simple to make and home-made means the ingredients are natural and pure, and occasionally freshly harvested.

Cordials and fruit syrups

Cordials are fruit syrups used to make drinks. The fresh fruit is cooked to a mash with a little water, strained, then sugar is added to the liquid that is boiled into a syrup. Occasionally I make a mango and orange syrup, which I enjoy poured over vanilla ice cream. Experiment with your cordials and create a new tradition for your family.

Muscatel Cordial

1kg gooseberries
1 litre water
10 heads elderflower blossom heads
1kg unbleached white sugar

Place the gooseberries in a saucepan, add the water and bring to the boil. Add the elderflowers and simmer gently for 5 minutes – you should have a greenish soupy mix. Set aside to cool. Strain the mixture through a muslin-lined sieve. Return the liquid to the saucepan and add the sugar. Bring to the boil, stirring constantly until completely melted. One the sugar has melted, boil for 4 minutes, taking care the syrup does not burn. Remove from the heat, pour into bottles, seal and store. Serve mixed with iced mineral or soda water.

Pear and Ginger Cordial

3kg pears
1 tablespoon thinly sliced fresh ginger
sugar

Roughly chop the pears and place in a large saucepan with just sufficient water to cover. Add the sliced ginger and bring to the boil, then simmer until soft enough to mash. Strain through a muslin-lined sieve. Measure the resulting liquid into a clean saucepan. Add an equal measure of sugar to the liquid. Bring to the boil, stirring constantly to dissolve the sugar. Boil for 3 minutes then remove from the heat, bottle and seal. Serve with fizzy or still mineral water.

Blackcurrant Cordial

2kg blackcurrants
sugar

Place the blackcurrants in a saucepan with 1 litre water. Measure the resulting liquid and add an equal measure of sugar. Bring to the boil and simmer until soft enough to mash. Strain through a muslin-lined sieve. Bring to the boil, stirring constantly to dissolve the sugar. Boil for 3 minutes then remove from the heat, bottle and seal.

When life's handing out lemons, make lemonade!

Squeeze the juice of a whole lemon into a pint glass, add a tablespoon of granulated sugar and half-fill the glass with cold water, stirring well to dissolve the sugar. Fill the glass to the brim with crushed ice. Stand for 3 minutes then drink.

Orangeade

juice of 4 oranges
rind of 2 oranges
50g sugar
1 litre cold water

Place all ingredients in a jug, stir well, add ice and serve.

ICE CREAMS AND SORBETS

I adore good ice cream. Before I owned an ice-cream maker I would freeze sorbets and ice creams in the fridge freezer, taking the chilling containers out every 15 minutes to mash and stir, working to prevent crystals. When the children were little and it snowed heavily or froze solid we made what we called 'proper home-made ice cream' – we would whip up cream and fold it into freshly made custard and often flavour it with jam from the larder and my son would take it out and tuck it in the snow, rushing out every 20 minutes or so to mash it up. Ice cream is a mixture of good custard, cream and flavouring.

Home-made Ice Cream Cones

These are fun to make especially if you've made your own ice cream. They used to impress my kids! They can be made ahead of time and stored in an airtight container for a week or so.

Sift together 100g cup plain flour, 60g caster sugar and 2 tablespoons cornflour. Add 60ml olive oil, 2 egg whites and 2 tablespoons cold water. Whisk together until there are no lumps.

Heat a heavy frying pan or griddle. Pour a tablespoon of mix into the hot pan, to make a flat 'pancake' 20cm wide. Fry quickly on both sides. Remove and immediately shape around a cardboard or metal cone shape. Leave for a couple of minutes to cool. Once cool the cones should hold their shape. Fill with a scoop of ice cream.

Almond and Apricot Ice Cream

300ml single cream
300ml plain yogurt
300ml soaked apricots, stewed with 100g sugar and puréed
100g ground almonds
100g roughly chopped almonds
2 tablespoons honey

Mix everything together well, then follow the freezing procedure used for Ginger Ice Cream.

Apple and Cinnamon Ice Cream

300g cooked apple purée
300ml single cream
300ml cold custard (see right)
2 teaspoons ground cinnamon
100g sugar

Mix everything together well, then follow the freezing procedure used for Ginger Ice Cream.

Ginger Ice Cream

My favourite ice cream. Leave out the ginger and syrup and you have vanilla ice cream fit for a princess.

4 egg yolks
100g sugar
300ml milk
½ teaspoon vanilla extract
20g cornflour
300ml double cream
half a 250g jar of ginger in syrup, coarsely chopped

1. To make the custard, place the egg yolks, sugar, milk, vanilla extract and cornflour in a bowl set over boiling water (or in a double boiler). Use a whisk to stir until thick and creamy (this will take between 10 and 15 minutes). Cover with a sheet of greaseproof paper and cool.

2. When the custard is quite cold, whip the double cream until peaking. Fold into the cold custard along with the chopped ginger and its syrup, pour into a freezer dish and place in the coolest part of the freezer. Remove every half hour and mash to get rid of ice crystals. If you have an ice-cream maker follow the manufacturer's instructions.

How to make a fruit sorbet

All you need to make a sorbet is whisked egg whites and fruit syrup or/and fruit purée and sugar. Use one stiffly whisked egg white and 225g caster sugar for every 450g syrup and purée. Fold all together and freeze. Remember to remove from the freezer regularly and if you don't have an ice-cream maker remove from the freezer every 20 minutes and mash away the ice crystals to create a smooth sorbet.

BAKING

A freshly baked Victoria sponge, sandwiched together with jam and cream, to be eaten with afternoon tea is a luxury few enjoy nowadays, along with freshly baked biscuits or cheese scones still warm from the oven, butter softly melting. Practise makes prefect.

Victoria Sponge

100g caster sugar
½ teaspoon vanilla extract
100g softened butter
2 large eggs
1 tablespoon water or milk
100g self-raising flour
two buttered 18cm cake tins

1 Preheat the oven to 190°C/375°F/gas mark 5.

2 Place the caster sugar, vanilla extract and softened butter in a large bowl. Using an electric whisk or wooden spoon mix well until the colour lightens and the mixture is creamy.

3 Add the eggs, one at a time, followed by the water, alternating with tablespoons of self-raising flour.

4 Divide the mixture between the two cake tins.

5 Bake for 20 minutes. Test by pushing a cocktail stick into the centre of each cake – the cocktail stick should come out quite clean. If so, tip the cakes onto a cake rack and leave to cool. If not, return to the oven for a further 5 minutes.

6 When cool, sandwich the layers together with home-made jam and sprinkle with caster sugar.

Home-made baking powder

To make the equivalent of 1 teaspoon commercial baking powder mix ½ teaspoon bicarbonate of soda, ½ teaspoon cream of tartar and ¼ teaspoon cornflour. Sift the mixture into a small bowl then add to flour.

Baking hints and tips

When buttering cake tins use clean fingers and soft butter. Sprinkle the buttered surface with plain flour and shake out the excess. This will ensure that cakes come out perfectly every time.

Have all ingredients at room temperature, including eggs.

Always sift dry ingredients together to ensure a perfect mix.

To cream butter and sugar easily start the process with butter softened to room temperature. Use a wire or electric whisk for best results. Perfectly creamed butter and sugar should be light and airy and a creamy colour.

When recipes call for ingredients to be folded in, use a metal spoon or a spatula for the purpose.

Always preheat the oven to the correct temperature.

Do not let cake mix stand too long before going in the oven as the baking powder will not be as effective.

If you don't have a cocktail stick handy to test whether a cake is baked through or not use a dry length of spaghetti.

summer

75

Sophie's Black Forest Gateau

Cherries, chocolate, cream and cake – what more could a girl want! And if the cherries have been preserved in brandy this becomes a very grown up cake.

225g softened butter
224g caster sugar
1 teaspoon vanilla extract

¼ teaspoon salt
175g self-raising flour
½ teaspoon baking powder
50g good cocoa powder
4 eggs
50ml milk
50ml water

Filling
500g jar stoned cherries in syrup
2 tablespoons cherry brandy
250ml double cream

Icing
100g dark chocolate
15g butter
1 tablespoon honey
50ml boiling water
30g sifted cocoa powder

1 Preheat the oven to 190°C/375°F/gas mark 5. Butter and flour a deep 18cm cake tin. Line with a disc of greaseproof paper to fit the base of the cake tin and drop in place.

2 Place the butter and sugar in a large mixing bowl and cream until light and fluffy. Add the vanilla extract and salt, whisk to mix. Then sift in the flour, baking powder and cocoa powder, eggs, milk and water. Use an electric whisk or a large metal spoon to mix into a thick, dropping consistency batter. Spoon into the prepared tin and bake for 50 minutes or until a knife inserted into the centre of the cake comes out clean. Turn out onto a cake rack to cool. When the cake is quite cold, cut into three layers.

3 Drain the cherries in syrup. Measure 4 tablespoons of syrup into a small bowl, add the brandy, stir well and spoon over the cake layers. Return the remaining syrup to the cherries. Whip the cream. Place the bottom cake layer on a serving plate. Spread with whipped cream and spoon over a third of the cherries in syrup. Put the middle layer in place and gently spread with cream and spoon over another third of the cherries. (Reserve a little of the cream for decorating.) Put the third layer in place and press lightly into place to settle the layers. Refrigerate the cake for 4 hours.

4 Melt the chocolate in a metal bowl set over a saucepan of boiling water (the bottom of the bowl should not touch the boiling water). Once melted remove from the heat, add the butter and honey, which should melt into the chocolate. Stir and add 50ml boiling water and the sifted cocoa powder. Immediately spread over the cake, covering the top layer and using a palette knife to spread around the sides. Leave for a few minutes to cool. Spoon the last of the whipped cream centrally on top of the cake and decorate with the last of the cherries in syrup.

Meringues

Makes 10 large, 20 medium or 30 small meringues

2 egg whites
100g caster sugar
50g icing sugar

Preheat the oven to 110°C/225°F/gas mark ¼.
Whisk the egg whites until they peak. Add half of
the sugar a spoonful at a time, whisking after each
spoonful. Pour in the remaining sugar and whisk.
Place spoonfuls on a baking tray covered with
baking parchment. Bake for between 1½ and
3 hours (depending on the size of the shapes).

Pavlova

4 large egg whites
200g caster sugar
pinch of salt
2 teaspoons cornflour
1 teaspoon vinegar

Preheat the oven to 150°C/300°F/gas mark 2.
Whisk the egg whites into stiff peaks. Add half the
caster sugar and the salt, a spoonful at a time,
whisk a little to mix after each additional spoonful.
Tip in the remaining caster sugar, whisk to mix
then fold in the cornflour and vinegar. Spoon the
mixture onto a parchment-lined baking tray,
shaping it in a circle with a slight indentation in
the centre. Bake for 50 minutes. Remove from the
oven and set aside to cool. When completely cold
decorate with whipped double cream flavoured
with a little kirsch, and summer berries.

Meringue Icing

2 egg whites
½ teaspoon cream of tartar
325g granulated sugar
125ml water
1 tablespoon lemon juice

Whisk the egg whites until frothy, add the cream
of tartar and continue whisking until peaking.
Measure the sugar and water into a saucepan and
slowly bring to the boil, stirring constantly to
dissolve the sugar. Boil for about 3 minutes then
test by dropping half a teaspoon of the syrup into
a bowl of cold water – a thread of syrup should
harden sufficiently to crack when dropped into the
water. Once this is reached switch off the heat.

Immediately set to whisking the egg whites and
pouring the syrup into the mix in a slow, steady
stream. Do not scrape the saucepan, just set it
aside once all that will pour out has, and continue
to whisk until the frosting is very thick and holds
its shape. This should take about 3 minutes (longer
if you are whisking by hand). Add the lemon juice
and whisk for a few seconds to mix in.

The icing should be used immediately. This icing
can be coloured with a couple of drops of food
colouring if you will. I usually divide it into
4 bowls, colouring each quarter differently, pink,
blue, green and yellow and drop generous blobs
onto cupcakes and sprinkle them with tiny white
icing stars or hundreds and thousands.

Lemon Meringue Pie

The perfect lemon meringue pie should consist of a just-baked, feather-light short pastry case filled with a deliciously lemony custard and topped with a lightly browned meringue.

Pastry
125g plain flour
50g softened butter
1 tablespoon iced water

1 Preheat the oven to 200°C/400°F/gas mark 6.

2 Sift the flour into a large mixing bowl, then use your fingertips to rub in the butter.

3 Add a little iced water to bring to a soft but firm dough. Refrigerate for 30 minutes to cool.

4 Butter a deep 20cm pie dish. Roll out the pastry to fit the pie dish. Prick the base a few times with a fork and bake blind in a hot oven for 15 minutes.

Filling
1 tablespoon cornflour
60g caster sugar
300ml milk
1 egg and 2 egg yolks
juice and rind of 2 lemons

1 Preheat the oven to 160°C/325°F/gas mark 3.

2 Place the cornflour and caster sugar along with a little of the milk in a bowl and stir until there are no lumps remaining. Add the remaining milk, egg and egg yolks. Stir well.

3 Set the bowl over a saucepan of simmering water and stir until the mixture is thick and creamy. Remove from the heat and add the lemon juice and rind. Taste. You may wish to add a little more sugar.

4 Pour the filling into the baked pastry shell and bake for 20 minutes until the filling is set. Remove and turn the oven down to 150°C/ 300°F/gas mark 2 in preparation for the meringue topping.

Meringue
2 egg whites
60g caster sugar

1 Whisk up the egg whites in a bowl until peaking. Add the caster sugar, a spoonful at a time, whisking lightly between spoonfuls.

2 When the filling has set, remove from the oven and spoon over the meringue mix. Use the spoon to shape over the pie. Bake for 10–15 minutes and serve immediately.

Perfect meringues

Things to remember when you make meringues:

The bowl and whisk should be spotlessly clean – the slightest hint of oil or butter will prevent the egg whites from whisking sufficiently.

Egg whites should be at room temperature, NEVER from the fridge.

Do not over-whisk the whites; stop whisking when the whites peak.

For very crisp meringues cook slowly at a low temperature.

For gooey, soft centred meringues add a touch more cornflour and a little vinegar.

If you don't have caster sugar, use granulated – it will take a little longer to dissolve but should be fine.

Some chefs swear by replacing a proportion of the sugar with icing sugar.

Use baking parchment on baking trays rather than buttering the trays.

WASH DAY

In Tudor times the washing women were known as 'lavenders'. In Victorian times the washer women would travel between the big houses, visiting every six weeks or so to boil and scrub, rinse and iron vast quantities of clothing and bed linen: coarse cottons, linens, handmade lace and, in the wealthy homes, the finest silks.

Washing smalls

Add 2 tablespoons soap flakes and 2 tablespoons borax to 3 litres warm water, mix well and soak delicate underwear. Wash gently and rinse well before hanging up to dry or drying flat.

Socks

No home is without an odd sock bag! To help reduce this international problem, only wash socks in pairs. Place pairs of socks in net wash bags. When washed, hang out to dry in pairs.

Crisp white sheets

A bed made up with crisp white sheets is a luxury we can all achieve, and one of my small indulgences. Good cotton sheets, well laundered, set to dry in the warm sun or a brisk breeze, ironed with fragrant lavender water and just a hint of starch, and then carefully folded and set to join the neat layers of linen in the airing cupboard, are a real pleasure. Good cotton sheets will also last a lifetime. Modern detergents work most efficiently, but be sure to double rinse to discourage detergent residue. A regular detergent-free wash using only half a cup of borax will keep whites white. Rinse out stains immediately with plenty of cold water and soap. Any accidental ironing scorch marks should be treated with a mixture of lemon juice and soap flakes, rinsed then put in the sun to dry.

Towels and sheets

Launder new towels and sheets before using, and hang out on the washing line to dry. If you favour natural cotton sheets, bring them in before they are completely dry, iron (I always use a little starch), place in airing cupboard or a clothes airer to air, then store. This will remove any commercial residues and, in the case of towels, eliminate fluff. Be sure to wash sets of towels or sheets together to ensure any resulting fading occurs at the same pace.

Handkerchiefs

Soak washed handkerchiefs in a solution of 1 teaspoon arrowroot, 1 teaspoon borax and 2 litres of near boiling water for 5 minutes. Squeeze and dry. When ironed the handkerchiefs should give off an agreeable fragrance.

Laundry essentials

Borax – to soften water

Bicarbonate of soda – stain removal

Scrubbing brush – to work at heavy fabrics

Soap flakes – for delicates and woollens

Laundry soap – for hand-washing

Rules

Always hand-wash bras and other good quality underwear, stockings and tights. Garments made from angora, cashmere, silk, chiffon, satin, lace and velvet should be washed individually with gentle detergent or a solution of soap flakes.

Do not wring out any of these fabrics, rather place on a clean towel, roll up loosely, pat dry and then open out.

If you intend laundering blankets or coats in the washing machine weigh them first to ensure your washing machine can cope with the quantity.

summer

81

Silk

Test for colourfastness by washing an inconspicuous area of the garment with a mild detergent solution and warm water, then pressing between two white cloths or tissues. If any colour transfers, soak the garment in a salt water solution as hot as the fabric will allow, rinse and dry. Test again.

If there are any spots, use a clean sponge dipped into the solution to gently rub the stain.

To rinse, soak the silk garment in a solution of 4 litres of cool water and 4 tablespoons of vinegar. The vinegar will help restore the characteristic shine to the silk.

Remove the garment from the rinse solution and lay flat on an absorbent towel. Roll the towel around the garment and squeeze gently to remove excess water. Unroll the towel and lay garment flat to dry.

Iron on the reverse side of the garment.

To launder silk ties

Boil a cup of bran in 2 litres of water for 5 minutes. Strain through muslin. Whilst the resulting liquid cools, spot clean the ties with a sponge and mild detergent. Lay ties one by one in the cooled liquid, pressing down gently with a clean sponge. Remove and lie between two towels, then press down with a rolling pin rolling along the length of the tie, pressing out as much liquid as possible. Dry flat, then iron over a clean cotton cloth.

Washing lace

Add a teaspoon of borax to warm soapy water when washing lace, stir and squeeze until quite clean. Rinse in cool water, and dry flat. Iron while damp.

How to wash pompoms

Make a good soapy mix of warm water, dip pompoms up and down 5 or 6 times, rinse in clean cold water and hang up to dry.

Denim jeans and jackets

Pull up zips and fasteners, turn inside out before washing. In hard-water areas, add 4 tablespoons of bicarbonate to the first rinse to soften the water, which will in turn aid rinsing.

The importance of washing lines

Hang washing out of doors to dry. The sun will naturally bleach whites white and dried laundry will smell fresh and clean. Towels and other heavy fabrics should be brought in before quite dry, ironed or folded and set to finish off over a clothes airer or in the airing cupboard.

To stiffen lace with rice water

Wash 2 tablespoons white rice in running water, drain, place in a saucepan with 2 litres cold water, boil for 5 minutes. Strain off the water. Soak the clean dry lace for 3 minutes in the rice water, remove, lay between two towels, press down to remove excess water, then iron the lace between two ironing cloths. The starch in the rice water should be sufficient to stiffen the lace.

Economy

Substitute half the stated quantity of powdered detergent for bicarbonate of soda.

For a smooth zip

To ease the path of a zip that sticks, rub the zip tracks with a pencil lead.

Keeping moths at bay

Epsom salts sprinkled amongst clothes whilst in storage will discourage moths.

Ironing essentials

Ironing board

Fragrant ironing water

Pressing cloths

Rectangle of old blanket to fold into shape to press awkward shapes.

Mending kit containing scissors, white and coloured threads, needles and a selection of buttons and other fasteners.

Soak dull or faded clothing in a solution of 1 cup distilled to 4 litres of fairly hot water for half an hour then put through the washing machine in the usual way but without any detergent.

Ironing board

Once a year re-cover your ironing board. Replace old padding with new, a couple of layers of old blanket fabric is ideal, followed by a layer of heavy calico and topped with pretty cotton fabric.

Fragrant ironing water

Fill a spray container with water, add a few drops of essential oil (lavender is lovely) and spritz cotton sheets and pillowcases as you iron.

Ironing awkward shapes

To iron a sleeve without making a crease, roll up a magazine, cover with a piece of padded cloth and insert into the sleeve. Let go and it should immediately unroll to the shape of the sleeve ready to iron.

To keep trouser creases in place, turn trousers inside-out and rub a piece of wet soap along the crease line. Turn right-way round and iron, using a damp cloth.

Ironing embroidery

Fold a blanket three or four times, lay over the ironing board and cover with a clean cloth. Place the embroidered fabric over the prepared area, cover with a second clean cotton cloth, spray lightly with water then iron. The heavy padding will enable the embroidered area to keep its shape.

Home-made Laundry Starch

Mix 100g white starch, 1 teaspoon borax and 1.8 litres cold water together using a whisk. Dip wet washed items into the starch and hang out dripping to dry.

Successful stain removal

I use a mixture of 'tried and true' and 'modern works best', thereby creating just a few new traditions of my own!

Non-oily nail varnish remover – use with a cotton bud to remove troublesome ink stains.

Suede – to remove grease spots use an old toothbrush and a little white vinegar, scrub gently and mop with a soft cloth.

Rust stains – moisten the spot with white vinegar and sprinkle with a little salt. Leave for a few minutes then work at the area gently with an old toothbrush. Rinse.

Collars and cuffs – paint with a bicarbonate of soda and vinegar paste an hour before laundering.

Perspiration smells and stains – soak in a mild solution of vinegar and water before laundering.

Ballpoint pen marks – use a paintbrush to apply methylated spirits, then rinse off after a few minutes; alternatively try a paste of white vinegar and cornflour.

To remove tea or coffee stains – soak the stained area in a strong borax solution before laundering.

summer

BATHING BEAUTY

I am addicted to bathing, just the thought of soaking in fragrant hot water, my hair piled up on my head, with a good book, the telephone and large fluffy towel waiting to do duty once the water has cooled. For me bath time is precious thinking time.

Bathe in milk and roses

A little summer luxury in a jar.

30g cocoa butter
10 drops attar of roses
30g finely grated good soap
150g ground oatmeal
1 tablespoon cream of tartar
1 tablespoon bicarbonate of soda

Place the cocoa butter in a china bowl set over a saucepan of boiling water until it has melted. Add 10 drops attar of roses and stir well. Set aside to cool. When the cocoa butter mixture is cold but not solid, place along with the remaining ingredients in a blender and mix well. Spoon into an attractive jar. Scoop two or three spoonfuls into a warm bath to enjoy a fragrant, skin-softening soak.

Bath Salts

Add half a cup of Epsom salts to a hot bath, sprinkle with rose petals and sink in for a relaxing bath.

Bath Vinegar

Add a handful of herbs to half a bottle of cider vinegar. Leave for a week before straining into a pretty bottle and add a few tablespoons to your bath.

Oatmeal and Almond Soak

100g oatmeal
100g ground almonds

Measure the ingredients into a bowl, mix well. Store in a glass jar. Add a few spoonfuls to a warm bath to soften the water and soothe your skin.

Herbal baths

Place a handful of herbs in a muslin bag and suspend from the hot tape when you bathe. Add:

Rosemary to stimulate

Mint to refresh

Thyme or sage when you are feeling a little under the weather

Lavender to relax and becalm

Lemon balm to raise the spirits

Rose petals for luxury

How to knit
a bath flannel

You will need a ball of double
knitting cotton yarn, a pair of
suitable knitting needles (check
this on the yarn label), a suitable
crochet hook and, if you want to
be fancy, a length of ribbon.

Taking up the needles and yarn,
cast on 3 stitches.

At the start of the next row and
each following row, cast on one
extra stitch.

When you have 50 stitches on
your knitting needles begin to
cast off, a single stitch at the end
of each row. When you have no
stitches left your flannel is almost
ready. Use the crochet hook and
yarn to crochet a simple border
around the flannel. You can also
thread ribbon in a decorative
fashion around the edge of your
flannel if you like.

Invigorating Salt and Olive Oil Body Scrub

Place 200g sea salt in a glass jar, add 60g lavender flowers and slowly pour in enough olive oil to cover; it will seep into the salt, so keep going until the level of olive oil is a centimetre above the salt mixture. Shake well. To use, stand in the bath and scoop out a handful of the mix, use a cotton mitt to apply to your skin, rubbing in circular movements over your entire body. Rinse well with hot water.

Bath Fizzies

4 tablespoons cocoa butter or coconut oil
2 tablespoons cream of tartar
4 tablespoons bicarbonate of soda
2 tablespoons cornflour
6 drops attar of roses
1 tablespoon dried rose petals

1 When you buy cocoa butter (or coconut oil) it is fairly solid in the pot. To melt it, place the jar in very hot water. While the cocoa butter is melting, measure and sift the dry ingredients into a bowl, then add the dried rose petals. When the cocoa butter has melted sufficiently to measure, take a spoonful, add 6 drops essential oil and pour into the dry mixture. Measure 3 further spoonfuls of cocoa butter into the dry ingredients. Stir to mix and after a few minutes you should have a ball of dough. You may need to add a little more oil, but don't add too much.

2 Tip the dough onto a clean surface and roll out to a thickness of 1cm. Cut into small hearts with a biscuit cutter. Place the shapes on a clean plate or baking tray and put them in the fridge for an hour to firm up. Store in labelled glass jars.

3 To use, place two or three fizzies in a hot bath. The little hearts will fizzle away leaving the water softened with the bicarb and fragrant with roses. The cocoa butter will soften, feed and smooth your skin.

Ginger Bath

Use sliced ginger in your bath to soothe stiffness in the joints and rheumatic pain. Cut a slice of ginger the size of a child's thumb. Slice thinly, bring to the boil in 1 litre water, simmer for 15 minutes then add the liquid to a warm bath.

AUTUMN

Autumn is the magical season. Rosehips and elderberries, the last few blackberries to be picked and before you know it there is a chill in the air and leaves turn from green to gold, and every shade in between. A hint of wood smoke sits in the air, sunlight thins and nature slows down. Damp days bring mushrooms and long country walks. It's time to gather nuts and tidy the garden, plant out bulbs and order seed catalogues.

ABUNDANCE

Use windfalls to make jellies and curds, or to freeze. Peel and discard any flesh that is the slightest bit brown or tainted. Lightly stew the prepared fruit in a little water and sugar to taste, then cool, pack into suitable pie-sized storage containers and freeze for use the whole year round.

Apples

There is a knack to harvesting apples. Take an apple in the palm of your hand and twist it slightly – if it comes away easily it is ready for picking, if not leave the apple to grow just a little longer. Apples don't all ripen at the same time; the ones at the top of the tree will ripen first.

Storing apples

Home-grown apples in good condition should be wrapped in squares of newspaper and stored on racks in a cool dry spot, away from mice or other vermin. They can be stored for up to four months.

Apple Rings

Peel and core apples, slice into rings about 5mm thick. Dip into a weak solution of lemon juice or vinegar and water to reduce discoloration. Thread the apple rings onto a length of string and hang above a range to dry. If you don't have a range, place the apple rings on racks and dry slowly in a barely warm oven with the door held slightly open to allow steam to escape. Once quite leathery, cool and store in a sealed container. Apple rings can be eaten as a snack or soaked in water and simmered gently before using in pies or sauces.

Toffee Apples

6 organic eating apples
500g granulated sugar
150ml water
2 teaspoons vinegar
80g butter
1 tablespoon golden syrup

Give the apples a good wash, dry, remove stalks and push in a sturdy stick. Measure the sugar and water into a saucepan. Bring slowly to the boil, stirring constantly. Add the vinegar, butter and golden syrup. Stir to mix and continue to boil.

Prepare a small bowl of cold water. After about 10 minutes, test the boiling mixture by dropping half a spoonful into the cold water. The mixture is ready when it goes quite hard once chilled in the water. When this stage is reached turn off the heat.

Half-fill a large bowl with very cold water. Take hold of the stick end of one of the apples, dip into the toffee mixture, twirling the stick to cover the apple. Continue to twirl until the apple has a reasonable layer of toffee over it, then remove. Dip it into the cold water, twirling a few times, then push it down on the base of the bowl to form the traditional stand shape. Remove and set down on a buttered surface to harden off.

Make a cake from courgettes

150g caster sugar

3 eggs

150ml olive oil

150g grated courgettes

300g plain flour

1 teaspoon baking powder

1 teaspoon bicarbonate of soda

pinch of salt

1 teaspoon ground cinnamon

juice and rind of 1 lemon

Preheat the oven to 190°C/375°F/gas mark 5. Measure the sugar, eggs and olive oil into a large bowl. Whisk until light and fluffy. Fold in all the remaining ingredients, beginning with the grated courgettes. Spoon the mixture into a prepared deep 20cm cake tin and bake for 45 minutes.

This mixture also works well baked as cupcakes!

Cinderella Soup

An economical soup fit for a princess.

If you have a large pumpkin you can make Cinderella Soup. Peel and chop enough pumpkin to half-fill a large saucepan. Cover with water and bring to the boil. Simmer until the pumpkin is soft. Remove from the heat. Either place the cooked pumpkin in a blender or mash in the cooking water until smooth. Add a crumbled vegetable stock cube and boiling water or some home-made stock to create a good thick soup. Warm over a low heat and season with salt and pepper. Serve with a good sprinkling of freshly chopped parsley and a large blob of yogurt.

Piccalilli

Makes 10 jars

2 cauliflowers

2 cucumbers

20 French beans

5 onions

1 garden marrow

2 teaspoons sea salt

1 litre vinegar

125g demerara sugar

25g whole spice

25g mustard powder

1 teaspoon mustard seeds

½ teaspoon ground pepper

1 teaspoon ground ginger

1 teaspoon ground turmeric

2 teaspoons cornflour

Chop the vegetables into small dice and put in a large china bowl. Sprinkle with the sea salt. Cover with a clean cloth and leave overnight.

Pour all but a cupful of the vinegar and the sugar and spices into a saucepan. Stir to dissolve the sugar. Bring to the boil. Drain off the liquid from the vegetables that has formed in the night and add the vegetables to the boiling mixture. Simmer for 10 minutes.

Pour the remaining cupful of vinegar into a small bowl, add the cornflour, mix well and pour into the simmering mix to thicken.

Continue cooking the piccalilli for 5 minutes. Taste for seasoning, adding more salt if necessary. Remove from the heat and bottle.

Pear Crisps, delicious to snack on

Choose near-ripe dessert pears. Slice thinly, leaving the skins on, and drop immediately into a solution of 4 tablespoons lemon juice and 4 tablespoons water. Shake dry and sprinkle with just a little caster sugar, then place on oiled racks and dry in the oven, heated to the coolest setting for about 4 hours. They are ready when they reach a leathery crispness. Cool and store in a sealed container. You can also make crisps from thinly sliced apples sprinkled with cinnamon and sugar in the same way.

Root vegetable crisps

Homemade crisps are best eaten the day you make them, but can be stored in an airtight container for up to a week. Do remember just how hot oil gets when deep frying. It is always best to use a purpose made deep fat fryer and follow manufacturer's directions. Parsnips, carrots, beetroot and potatoes all make good crisps. Give the vegetables a good scrub and dry with a clean tea towel. Use a mandolin to slice the vegetables thinly, 20–30mm is about right. Too thin and the crisps burn, too thick and they don't crisp up! Fry a few at a time, when cooked remove from the oil and place on a kitchen towel to soak up excess oil, then onto a plate and sprinkle with sea salt.

Roast sunflower seeds

Toss a handful of peeled sunflower seeds into a heavy bottomed frying pan, sprinkle with soy sauce and cook for a few minutes. Tip into a bowl and enjoy.

Roasting pumpkin

To roast pumpkin, simply peel and chop into fairly large pieces, sprinkle with olive oil and sea salt and roast in a hot oven until brown around the edges and tender. Roasting intensifies the flavour of pumpkin.

Perfect Pumpkin Pie

Shortcrust pastry (*see p.110*)

Filling
250g peeled and chopped pumpkin
1 teaspoon ground cinnamon
½ teaspoon ground mixed spice
2 large eggs
75g sugar
200ml double cream

1 Preheat the oven to 180°C/350°F/gas mark 4.

2 Butter a deep 20cm pie dish. Roll out the pastry to fit the pie dish. Prick the base a few times with a fork and bake blind for 15 minutes.

3 Steam the pumpkin until tender, then place in a bowl and mash in the spices.

4 Separate the eggs. Place the yolks in a bowl with the sugar and whisk until light and fluffy.

5 Place the egg whites in a bowl and whip until light and peaking.

6 Stir the cream into the now cooled mashed pumpkin and spice mixture. Mix well. Add the egg yolk and sugar mixture, stirring well. Fold in the whipped egg whites and pour the mixture into the cooked pastry case.

7 Bake for 35 minutes or until a knife, when inserted, comes out clean. Serve warm with cream.

Borscht

In Poland, every cook has a different recipe for borscht. Some add tomatoes, others don't; some use leeks, others only onions. The mixture of green herbs varies according to area and season. I use a traditional recipe, given to me by a Polish woman. She told me it was her grandmother's recipe.

Like so many recipes it begins with onions. Chop and fry 3 onions. Add 2 large scrubbed and grated carrots, a bunch of beetroots, scrubbed and grated, wash the tops and chop, add to the mix. If you have leeks, slice thinly and add to the mix. Place a lid on the pan and allow to cook gently for 10 minutes. Next, add one can of chopped tomatoes (or if you have them, 6 chopped tomatoes), 2 medium potatoes, thinly peeled and cubed, 1 litre of vegetable stock. Now the spices: add 5 cloves and a few allspice berries, half a cup of chopped parsley and a couple of sprigs of oregano or marjoram. Allow to simmer gently for an hour and serve with a dollop of yogurt or sour cream and thick slices of warm, crusty wholemeal bread. Vodka is not obligatory.

FISH AND SEAFOOD

My grandfather was a fisherman but my Uncle Jack's speciality was crayfish, which he would catch on a Sunday morning, when the tide was right. Later that day we would sit at the table and eat freshly cooked crayfish. Warm and tender, dripping with melted butter and just a sprinkling of salt.

The fish man

Once everyone had a fish man. He travelled a weekly route, his little van loaded down with fresh fish on ice. There would be a knock at the back door and there he would stand with a small white paper-wrapped parcel containing ingredients for a fish pie or a couple of skate wings, possibly a nice piece of haddock, filling your regular order with a 'will there be anything else this week, I've got some lovely whiting/Dover sole/herrings on ice, just in this morning'. Ah – those were the days...nowadays we stand at the fish counter, spoilt for choice and often wondering just what to do with it if we get it home!

How to make a fish pie

I usually buy a salmon steak, and equal quantity of smoked cod or haddock and an economically priced white fish, also a good handful of peeled prawns.

Serves 2 (with enough leftovers for a light lunch)

1 Preheat the oven to 180°C/350°F/gas mark 4.

2 Peel, cook and mash 4 medium potatoes. While the potatoes are cooking cut the fish into bite-sized pieces. Put the fish (NOT the prawns) into a saucepan and cover with milk. Bring gently to the boil, turn down immediately and simmer gently until the fish is just cooked. Remove from the stove and strain the milk into a small bowl.

3 Make a little white sauce using 250ml of the drained milk. To do this, splash about a tablespoon of olive oil or butter in a small saucepan, add a tablespoon of plain flour and a sprinkling of salt and pepper. Mix over a low heat, cook for a minute or two then pour in the milk stirring constantly. Once it is thick, remove from the heat and pour over the fish and prawns and a good tablespoon of freshly chopped parsley and a squeeze of lemon juice. Tip all into a suitable baking dish, cover with a thick layer of mashed potato and sprinkle with breadcrumbs and if you have it handy, a little grated cheese (but I don't always do this!). Bake for 20 minutes, then serve with vegetables or a good green salad.

Poach a whole salmon

Clean and scale the salmon. Wash well in cold water. Place the salmon in a fish kettle or in a large, deep baking container (a roasting tin would do admirably). If you do not have a container large enough to lay the fish out flat you should curl it in the shape of the container. Cover with cold water to which you have added a good splash of olive oil, a sliced lemon and a small bunch of parsley. Cover with the lid or well tucked in heavy aluminium foil. Place on the stove and bring to a very gentle simmer. The water should barely move. To measure the cooking time, weigh the fish and allow 10 minutes plus 20 minutes for every kilo. To check that the fish is cooked pull at the dorsal fin – if it comes out easily the fish is cooked. Remove from the cooking liquid, rest for 15 minutes then serve hot, or set aside until quite cold before serving cold.

My Hollandaise Sauce

Place 2 egg yolks, 50g butter, a good splash of olive oil, salt and pepper to taste and the juice and rind of half a lemon in a bowl. Set the bowl above a saucepan of simmering water and whisk until thick and creamy adding a little stock to thin slightly. Serve at once.

Home-made Fish Stock

fish heads and tails from 3 or 4 small fish or 1 large fish
1 onion
2 carrots
2 celery sticks
1 leek
a little parsley
1 bay leaf
3 peppercorns

Pour 3 litres water into the saucepan. Chop up all the vegetables and place them in the saucepan with the water. Add the fish heads, tail and bones, parsley, bay leaf and peppercorns. Place the saucepan on the cooker and bring to the boil, reduce the temperature and cook at a gentle simmer with the lid on for about an hour. Remove from the heat, strain and the stock is ready to use.

Pickled Fish

This is a quintessentially South African dish.
Take 2kg firm white fish, chop into bite-sized pieces and toss in flour. Next slice 4 large onions and fry in a little oil; when soft and cooked but not coloured, add 2 level teaspoons garam masala, a level teaspoon turmeric, a pinch of cloves, a squeeze of lemon and sprinkle on a teaspoon of sugar. Drop in 2 or 3 bay leaves and if you have them, some curry leaves, one very small chilli and 6 peppercorns. Sprinkle with salt to taste and finally add 200ml vinegar and simmer gently. Add the fish and simmer until cooked. Pickled fish is best eaten a day after cooking. Eat with bread and salad.

autumn

99

Soused Herrings

Pour 200ml of cider vinegar in a shallow baking dish. Slice one large onion thinly and spread half the onion rings across the base of the dish, in the vinegar. Take 6 fresh herrings, fillet and wash, sprinkle liberally with sea salt and black pepper, roll and set comfortably in the vinegar. Sprinkle the whole with one coarsely chopped chilli (seeds removed) and a teaspoon of juniper berries, tucking some between the fillets. Toss the remaining onion rings across the top of the dish and cover with a lid or foil. Bake in a medium oven for 40 minutes, remove the lid and return to the oven for a further 15 minutes. Cool and serve with brown bread and butter, fresh coleslaw and a green salad.

How to smoke fish

It is quite possible to smoke fish in your kitchen. Smoking does generate smoke, so prepare by opening a window and setting a spot just out of doors where you can place the smoking tray once removed from the heat. I would recommend starting with either trout fillets or salmon steaks. The fish will have a delicate smoked flavour.

½ teaspoon sea salt
1 teaspoon lemon juice
1 tablespoon olive oil
150ml cold water
4 trout fillets
salt and freshly ground black pepper
large handful wood chippings (ideally made from alder or oak)

1 Make a marinade with the sea salt, lemon juice, olive oil and water in a shallow bowl. Place the trout fillets in the marinade, cover and store in the refrigerator for 1 hour.

2 To prepare your smoker place a layer of heavy-gauge aluminium foil in the roasting tin then lay a handful of wood chippings on the bottom. Oil the rack and place it on top of the tray. The rack should rest sufficiently above the wood chippings so nothing is touching.

3 Remove the fillets from the marinade and place on the rack, skin side down. Cover the entire tray with a double layer of heavy-gauge aluminium foil. Tuck the ends tightly over to ensure a good seal. The foil should not be touching the fish.

4 Open a window! Place the tray over the highest gas flame your cooker has and leave it there for 3 minutes. Switch off the gas and leave for a few minutes.

5 Open the foil (I usually take the whole baking tray outside before I open it) and the trout should be cooked through. It will have turned a lovely orangey shade and taste smoked. Serve with a salad lunch.

When smoking salmon fillets, lay fennel tops across the wood chippings.

If you have difficulty obtaining suitable wood chippings, try using 3 tablespoons uncooked rice and a teaspoon of sugar along with some fennel greens from the garden. In the Scandinavian countries salmon is smoked out of doors over juniper branches and hot coals.

Some woods are poisonous so take care not to smoke fish over anything but untreated wood chippings specifically prepared for smoking food.

How to pot shrimps

When it comes to potted shrimps those little brown English shrimps are best. Salt and pepper and nutmeg and mace, a little lemon juice and you have a dish fit for a queen.

Serves 2 for lunch, or 4 as a starter

100g butter
pinch of nutmeg
pinch of mace
250g cooked and peeled shrimps
2 teaspoons lemon juice
salt and white pepper to taste

Melt the butter gently in a small saucepan. Add the nutmeg and mace and stir.

Toss the peeled shrimps in the lemon juice then add them to the melted butter mixture, stirring gently to ensure all the shrimps are covered with the mixture.

Season to taste with salt and white pepper.

Spoon into prepared ramekins or small jars. Spoon any remaining butter over shrimps to cover. Set in the fridge to cool.

Serve with a lettuce and tomato salad and sliced brown bread and butter.

Maryland Crab Cakes

Best made from fresh Maryland Blue crabmeat, but can be made with just about any other fresh or chilled chunky crabmeat.

Serves 2

50g cream crackers
1 egg
2 tablespoons mayonnaise
good squeeze of lemon juice
sea salt and black pepper
500g white and brown crabmeat
oil for frying

Whizz the crackers in a blender or place them in a plastic bag and crush into breadcrumbs.

Lightly whisk the egg, mayonnaise, lemon juice and salt and pepper in a large bowl, add the crabmeat and crumbs and mix well. Set aside for 20 minutes to firm up.

Take a generous tablespoon at a time and shape into thick, slightly flattened cakes. Refrigerate while you prepare the salad and lay the table.

Fry in a little oil, turning once. Finished crab cakes should be golden brown.

Serve with crispy bread, a green salad, a large bowl of potato salad and freshly made caper and lemon mayonnaise.

Eating mussels

Mussels are incredibly quick and easy to prepare and cook, and in the distant past were widely eaten by rich and poor. Nowadays people can be just a little nervous of choosing and preparing mussels but there is very little to it.

Buy mussels from a reliable source. Choose mussels that look fresh and healthy, shiny shells that are not broken or chipped.

Cook on the same day or within a day or two of purchase. Immediately you get home with your mussels tip them into a container of clean cold water with a sprinkling of plain flour and place in the fridge. Throw away any mussels that don't close tightly when placed in the cold water.

To prepare, remove one at a time and scrape and scrub away any hairy bits. Discard any mussels with cracks or holes. A quick rinse in cold water and they are ready to cook.

For a kilo of mussels you will need a large saucepan and a good splash of olive oil. Add a sliced onion and a couple of garlic cloves, then fry gently. When cooked, pour in a wine glass of dry white wine, bring to the boil, then tip in the mussels, put the lid on and give a bit of a shake. Leave for a minute or two and the mussels should be cooked. Shake, then check and possibly give them another 30 seconds. Mussels are cooked when the shells are all open to reveal their meaty filling (discard any that won't open). Once the mussels are cooked, lift them out into warm bowls. Add half a wine glass of cream to the cooking liquid and a tablespoon or so of chopped parsley. Warm gently, while stirring, then pour over the cooked mussels. Serve with plenty of warm crusty bread to mop up the juices.

GAME

The arrival of autumn means once more we can include game on the menu. Pheasant, quail and partridge (my personal favourite). As I live on my own, I often roast a partridge just for one, and serve it with roast pumpkin, root vegetables and a rich gravy.

To cook a rabbit

Place the whole rabbit in a large saucepan along with an onion and a carrot and bring to the boil, simmer gently with the lid on for 2 hours, or until the flesh drops off the bone. Remove from the heat, drain and discard the liquid and vegetables. Remove all the meat from the bones, taking care as rabbit bones are small.

Poacher's Pie

Serves 4

Pastry
200g plain flour
100g lard
cold water

Filling
1 onion, chopped
1 medium carrot, diced
2 tablespoons freshly chopped parsley
½ teaspoon mixed dried herbs
2 medium potatoes, peeled and chopped
150ml vegetable stock
handful of peas
400g cooked rabbit meat
200g sausage meat

To make up the pastry, mix the flour and lard with your fingertips until the mixture resembles breadcrumbs, then bring the pastry together with a little cold water. Place in the fridge to rest for half an hour.

Preheat the oven to 190°C/375°F/gas mark 5.

Fry the onion in a little oil, then add the diced carrot. Sprinkle with the parsley and mixed herbs and toss in the chopped potatoes. Add the vegetable stock. Spoon into a deep pie dish, add the peas, cooked rabbit meat and sausage meat, broken up into lumps. Stir all well together and press down into place. Roll out the pastry and shape into a lid, place over the filling and seal. Decorate with pastry leaves and make a hole in the centre for the steam to escape. Paint the pastry lid with a little milk or eggwash.

Bake for 30 minutes then reduce the temperature to 180°C/350°F/gas mark 4 for a further 30 minutes. Serve hot.

Quail Salad

Serves 2

2 oven-ready quail
soy sauce
200g small cooked salad
   potatoes
bowl of salad leaves
olive oil
balsamic vinegar
salt and freshly ground
   black pepper
capers

Set two frying pans on the stove each containing a little olive oil. Divide the quail into breasts and legs, toss in a little soy sauce and fry in hot olive oil until cooked pink. Saute the potatoes in the second frying pan. While all is cooking, dress the salad leaves with olive oil, tossing to cover all the leaves, and sprinkle with just a little good balsamic vinegar. Place a large handful of prepared leaves on each of two plates. Add the quail meat, tearing the breasts into 2 or 3 pieces and set the cooked legs at an attractive angle amidst the leaves. Sprinkle all with a few capers and serve.

autumn

105

How to make good use of a whole chicken

First roast your chicken stuffed with plenty of sage and onion stuffing. Portion up slices of roast chicken along with a drumstick or wing on each plate along with a good serving of stuffing, plenty of roast potatoes, seasonal vegetables and lots of rich gravy.

Back in the kitchen remove all the meat from the carcass and place in a covered bowl in the fridge to be cooked in a pie with a tasty white wine sauce and lots of mushrooms, or in a chicken and mushroom risotto. Save the carcass to make Chicken Broth with Dumplings or Chicken Noodle Soup.

CHICKEN

In days gone by every cottager would keep a few hens, for both eggs and the pot – when a hen went into the pot you can be sure nothing went to waste. A good free-range chicken stuffed and roasted will feed a family, with enough meat on the bones to make a nutritious chicken broth.

Roast Chicken with Sage and Onion Stuffing

Serve with roast potatoes and vegetables.

Choose a good plump chicken, 1.5 to 2kg in weight. Remove the giblets and, if you are lucky, the feet and place in a small saucepan along with a bay leaf and a little parsley. Bring to the boil then simmer with the lid on for 30 minutes. Set aside.

Stuffing
1 medium carrot, grated
1 medium onion, finely chopped
a little olive or sunflower oil
250g breadcrumbs or oatmeal
250g sausage meat
1 egg
2 tablespoons freshly chopped parsley
1 teaspoon freshly chopped sage leaves (or ½ teaspoon dried sage)
1 teaspoon freshly chopped thyme (or ½ teaspoon dried thyme)
good pinch of salt
freshly ground black pepper

1 Preheat the oven to 200°C/400°F/gas mark 6.

2 Fry the carrot and onion in a little oil until soft. Place the oatmeal (or breadcrumbs), sausage meat, egg, herbs and seasoning in a mixing bowl. Add the cooked onion and carrot. Using your hands mix thoroughly.

3 Give the bird a quick wash, inside and out. Fill the cavity of the chicken with stuffing. Any stuffing left over should be shaped into balls and set aside. Rub the skin of the bird with a little oil and sprinkle with salt. Place in a roasting pan and pop into a hot oven for 20 minutes for every 450g, plus an additional 20 minutes extra for the bird (if the chicken is not stuffed this becomes 15 minutes for every 450g and an extra 15 minutes for the bird).

Place an apple in the cavity of a pheasant or partridge when roasting for a deliciously juicy roast.

autumn

Home-made Chicken Stock

Nowadays stock comes in cubes or sachets. Our grandmothers had a stockpot!

There isn't an exact recipe for stock but there are a few no no's. Apart from parsley stalks, don't add herbs, don't add potatoes or the stock will be cloudy, and be sure to strain the stock well.

a cooked or raw chicken carcass or chicken bones or chicken wings
1 onion
2 carrots
2 celery sticks
1 leek
a little parsley
1 bay leaf
3 peppercorns

Pour 3 litres water into the saucepan with the chicken carcass. Chop up all the vegetables and add them to the water. Add the parsley, bay leaf and peppercorns. Place the saucepan on the stove and bring to the boil, reduce the temperature and cook at a gentle simmer with the lid on for about an hour. Remove from the heat, strain and the stock is ready to use.

If you are not going to use the stock immediately then you can store it in the fridge in clean containers for up to 4 days, or freeze and use within 3 months. Remember to label your containers clearly.

The Chicken Moist Maker

(As opposed to the Turkey Moist Maker)

2 medium slices of good wholemeal bread
warmed leftover gravy
slices of leftover stuffing

Butter the bread and pour a little warmed gravy over the bottom slice, spread with slices of cold stuffing and possibly a few morsels of chicken, add a little more warmed gravy, season with salt and pepper and cover with a slice of bread.

Chicken Broth with Dumplings

Place the chicken carcass in a saucepan, with a small chopped onion, and a couple of celery sticks, chopped, 2 small carrots, a piece of lemon rind, a few sprigs of parsley and a little lemon thyme. Add 1.5 litres water, bring to the boil and simmer with the lid on for an hour or so. Drain off the broth and return it to the pan. Add any bits of leftover chicken and bring to the boil. Add the prepared dumplings and cook with the lid on until the dumplings are cooked through.

Dumplings
20g softened butter
100g self-raising flour
1 tablespoon finely chopped fresh parsley
¼ teaspoon finely chopped lemon thyme
a little milk

To make, rub the butter into the flour, add the herbs and bring it all together with a little milk. Shape into small balls, no bigger than a large marble.

Good Old-fashioned Chicken Soup

Place a chicken carcass in 2 litres of water along with a bay leaf, a bunch of fresh parsley, 4 peppercorns, a little thyme and 6 cloves of garlic. Simmer gently with the lid on for 1 hour. Strain and serve.

Chicken Noodle Soup

My childhood is full of bowls of Chicken Noodle Soup – try it. Make up the chicken broth as for Chicken Broth with Dumplings and instead of the dumplings add a handful of broken up Chinese noodles just before serving, simmer for a couple of minutes for them to cook and serve with hot buttered toast.

Hay box cooking

In long gone days during hard times, or when fuel was scarce, or whole families went out to work and there was no one left at home to prepare an evening meal, a stew would be prepared in a pot, started over the fire or stove, then the pot would be placed in a large box on a layer of hay. More hay would be packed tightly around and over the pot, creating a nest. Finally a lid would go over the top and the box set aside, the stew would continue cooking in the insulated warmth. In the evening there would be a hot meal ready.

Chicken Baked in Hay

Cooking a chicken in hay brings the flavour of the harvest to the food, and keeps the chicken moist. Set a pot of water on the stove containing the chicken giblets and feet, one roughly chopped onion and a carrot, along with some celery to make stock for the gravy.

small bag of fresh, clean hay
small bunch thyme
good roasting chicken
butter, salt and pepper
250ml water

Preheat the oven to 200°C/400°F/gas mark 6.

Soak the hay and a few sprigs of thyme in cold water for two hours.

Prepare the chicken, then rub it with butter and dust with salt and pepper, inside and out. Place 4 sprigs of thyme in the cavity along with a little butter.

Place a third of the hay in the bottom of a large oven dish. Lay the chicken on top then tuck soaked hay and thyme sprigs around the bird and on top.

Pour a cup of water over the hay-covered chicken. Cover the oven dish and place in the oven.

Bake for 1½ hours. Remove the covered dish from the oven. Lift off the hay and discard, then remove the chicken from the hay nest and place it in a clean roasting dish. Return to the oven uncovered for a few minutes to brown. Prick between the thigh and body to ensure the chicken is cooked – if it is, the juices will run clear.

PASTRY

My grandmother made beautiful pastry; she used chilled soda water to make shortcrust pastry and when she made puff pastry the layers were folded with strict precision.

How to always make good pastry

The first time I cooked for the 60-strong community at Old Hall in Suffolk, I remember a few of the members advising me that anything with pastry was a bad idea as it was not possible to make good pastry with wholemeal flour. Well, I used my grandmother's secrets, baked pies and the plates were licked clean.

So…be sure that all the ingredients are cool (including the flour), cube the butter before tossing it in the flour and once your pastry is made, shape into a short, thick slab, place on a covered plate and put into the fridge to cool for at least half an hour. When rolling out the pastry use as few strokes as possible. Oh, and if you have any pastry left over, be sure to roll it out and place into a suitable baking tray, bag and freeze to use at a later date. Pastry can be shaped into individual tart tins or, if you have sufficient, into layer cake tins.

Shortcrust Pastry

Makes 22cm pastry shell

240g plain flour
125g butter
tablespoon or two of iced water

Sift the flour into a large mixing bowl. Cut the butter into 1cm cubes and drop into the flour. Using only your fingertips, rub the butter into the flour and continue until the mixture comes together; you will need to add a tablespoon or two of iced water, but don't add too much. Shape into a short thick slab, and refrigerate for half an hour. Remove from the fridge, dust a clean surface with flour and roll the pastry to the required thickness and place in well-buttered and floured baking tins. Return the pastry cases to the fridge for 15 minutes before baking.

If you would like to make a sweet shortcrust pastry suitable for jam tarts or to fill with chocolate custard or fruit in syrup, add 3 level tablespoons caster sugar to the shortcrust recipe.

Baking blind

To bake blind is to bake the pastry case without a filling. Butter the pie tin and roll out the pastry, lay it in the tin and trim away any excess. Cut a piece of greaseproof paper to shape and lay it across the pastry. Spread a layer of dried butter beans or specially made baking beans across the paper. Bake the pastry until crisp and cooked through, then remove from the oven. The beans can be used time and time again – store them in a labelled jar.

Rough Puff Pastry

250g plain flour
125g butter
125g softened butter
3 tablespoons iced water
1 teaspoon lemon juice

1 Sift the flour into a mixing bowl.

2 Cube 125g butter, add to the flour and rub in, using your fingertips.

3 Mix in the iced water and lemon juice and form into a short thick slab.

4 Dust your work surface with a little flour and lay the pastry in the centre. Roll into a rectangle about 5mm thick. Spread with half of the 125g softened butter. Gently fold the pastry one third up from the bottom of the rectangle and one third down from the top of the rectangle, creating three layers. Place in the fridge for 15 minutes. Remove and once again lay on a flour dusted surface. As before, roll out into a rectangle. Spread with the remaining butter and repeat the two folds. Refrigerate for half an hour and your pastry will be ready to use. This is not puff pastry, but it certainly will puff and should have a certain amount of flake.

Jessie Judge's Famous Kalgoolie Beef Pasties

Meat pie crusts can become sodden and soft after settling into the gravy during cooking. To avoid this, place four skewers across a dish and lay the pie crust over them. When you take the pie from the oven, remove the skewers, then pour a little extra gravy into the steam holes.

As made by Jessie and her mother before her. This recipe comes from another of the colonies: Australia. Jessie's pasties played a large part in my brother-in-law Peter's culinary education! Made with home-made rough puff pastry, rolled out and cut into large circles, these pasties are filled with a mixture of grated potato and grated swede to which a generous helping of chopped parsley is added along with top quality cubed beef steak seasoned with salt and pepper.

Place the filling down the centre of the pastry circles, eggwash the edges of the pastry and bring up on either side of the filling to join in a spine that runs over the top of the pasty. Seal well, brush with eggwash and bake for 20 minutes in a hot oven, reducing the temperature for a further 40 minutes. Serve with tomato or brown sauce.

Cornish Pasties

My South African grandfather, Scotty Waters, was born in Cornwall and most proud of his Cornish heritage; he loved the sea, was a natural boatman and an excellent fisherman. When he was in my grandmother's good books she would treat him to her version of home-made Cornish pasties for supper.

Serves 4

Pastry made with 500g plain flour and a pinch of salt, 250g lard and iced soda water to mix (*see p.110*)

The stew
1 large onion, chopped
400g cubed lamb fillet
salt and pepper
pinch of mace
1 large carrot, chopped and
    cooked
1 tablespoon plain flour
1 tablespoon fresh parsley,
    chopped
rich meat stock

1   Fry the chopped onions in a little oil. Add the cubed lamb and fry to seal. Sprinkle with the mace, salt and pepper. Toss in the chopped cooked carrot. Remove from the pan and set aside. Add a little more oil or butter to the pan, sprinkle with the flour and chopped parsley, mix well, scraping away at any bits sticking to the bottom of the pan, and add a couple of cupfuls of stock. Stir until you have a good glossy gravy. Set aside to cool, covered with a sheet of greaseproof paper.

2   Preheat the oven to 220°C/425°F/gas mark 7.

3   When it is time to cook the pasties, roll out the dough and cut 4 side-plate sized circles of pastry. Paint milk or eggwash around the edge of the first pastry circle, spoon the lamb and vegetable mixture onto one side of the circle, but not too much. Arrange the mixture to create an empty spot in the centre of the meat (later you will pour gravy into this spot, and the meat will support the shape of the pastry). Fold the pastry over to cover the filling, using a fork and your fingertips to seal the join. Place carefully on a prepared baking tray. When you have prepared all four of the pasties and they are set on the baking tray, use a funnel to add a little of the gravy to each pasty – not much, just a tablespoon or so.

4   Bake for 20 minutes in the hot oven then reduce the heat to 160°C/325°F/gas mark 3 and bake for a further 30 minutes (larger pasties will need a longer cooking time than smaller ones). Heat up the remaining gravy and, once you have the pasties plated up along with vegetables and mashed or boiled potatoes, use a funnel to carefully fill the pasties with hot gravy. Pour remaining gravy into a warmed jug or gravy boat and place on the table.

SWEETIES AND BAKING

Back in the old days, when we were girls at school, my Aunt Heather was the fudge queen of St Mary's, Kloof. Along with a few of the other stay-at-home mums, she ran the school tuck-shop. Her fudge was famous, along with her coconut ice, cakes, crunchies and the rest.

Home-made Honeycomb

Deliciously crunchy honeycomb toffee is simple yet dramatic in creation! My grandmother used to make it, insisting I stood well back as she poured the foaming mixture onto a buttered baking tray. If you have a large marble slab or marble kitchen surfaces, you can turn the foaming honeycomb out directly on it instead of a baking tray.

1 tablespoon bicarbonate of soda
200g sugar
4 tablespoons golden syrup

Butter a baking tray or other suitable surface. Measure out the bicarbonate of soda and have a hand whisk ready.

Place sugar and syrup in a medium-sized, heavy-bottomed saucepan. Place the saucepan over a lowish heat and stir the mixture with a wooden spoon as it melts. Once melted, remove the spoon and watch as the mixture simmers until it is bubbling and golden (this should only take 3 or 4 minutes).

Remove from the stove and whisk in the bicarbonate of soda. The mixture will erupt like a volcano, foaming up almost frighteningly.

Pour onto the buttered baking tray, or marble surface. Leave to cool then break into suitable-sized splinters for dipping in chocolate or crumbling into ice cream.

Butterscotch

500g sugar
125ml milk
3 tablespoons water
85g butter
pinch of cream of tarter

Measure all the ingredients into a saucepan, place on the stove and bring to the boil, stirring until the sugar has dissolved. Boil until the syrup reaches soft-crack stage. Check by dropping a spoonful of the syrup into a bowl of very cold water – it should form a thread that easily snaps. Once this stage is reached, pour it into a buttered tin. When nearly set mark into squares; break when cold and wrap in sweet papers.

Boiling sugar

Soft-ball 115°C

Test by dropping into cold water; it should be able to hold a small ball shape.

Hard-ball 120°C

Test in cold water; it should roll into a larger, harder ball than soft-ball.

Soft-crack 125°C

Test in cold water; it should be brittle, but still sticky on the fingers.

Hard-crack 146°C

Test in cold water; it should be very brittle with no stickiness.

How to make waffles

2 eggs
125ml milk
250g plain flour
3 teaspoons baking powder
125ml water
25g butter

Separate the eggs. Place the yolks in one bowl, the whites in another. Add the milk to the egg yolks, mix well, then sift in the flour and baking powder. Whisk together until there are no lumps, add the water, whisk to mix. Whisk the egg whites until stiff and peaking. Fold into the batter. Melt the butter and fold into the mixture.

Waffle irons do not need oiling. Simply heat then sprinkle a little water on the hot plate and close. When the iron steams it is hot enough to make waffles. Spoon sufficient batter over the waffle iron to fill (you will need less than you think!). Waffles taste best just cooked, however if you are in the mood, cook a batch of waffles and freeze. To warm simply defrost and place in the toaster to heat up. Serve with honey or jam or, best of all, quince jelly (*see p.120*).

This batter can be used to make scrumptious South African crumpets (similar to American-style pancakes). Heat a frying pan, wipe with the tiniest bit of oil or butter and when good and hot cook tablespoon quantities of batter over a medium heat until the bubbles burst. Turn them over and cook until golden on the second side. Serve with butter and jam or honey, or American style with bacon and eggs.

How to make scones

The trick to light scones is to handle the dough as little as possible, then bake hot and quick. A perfect scone should rise wonderfully and split easily in two without a knife. Scones should be eaten within a couple of hours of baking.

Makes 8 scones

250g plain flour
4 teaspoons baking powder
50g butter
125ml milk

Preheat the oven to 220°C/425°F/gas mark 7.

Sift the flower and baking powder into a mixing bowl. Cut the butter into small cubes and toss into the flour, then using only your fingertips rub the butter into the flour until the mixture resembles breadcrumbs. Add the milk, a little at a time and use a spatula or blunt-ended knife to mix into a soft dough. Tip onto a floured surface and pat into an oblong about a 1.5cm thick. Use a round biscuit cutter dipped in flour to cut the scones. Place gently on a buttered baking tray and bake for 12 minutes. Cool and serve with jam and cream.

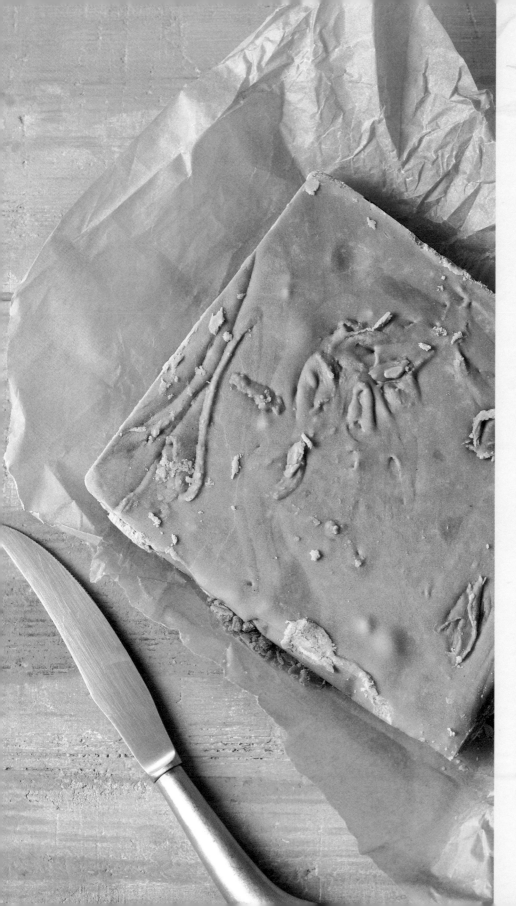

Heather Holt's Vanilla Fudge

**2kg, plus 4 tablespoons
sugar
1 tin condensed milk
125ml milk
120g butter or margarine
1 tablespoon golden syrup
1 teaspoon cocoa powder
1 teaspoon vanilla essence**

Measure everything but the
condensed milk and vanilla
essence into a large
saucepan. Bring to the boil
slowly, stirring to melt the
sugar. Add the condensed
milk and turn up the heat.
Stir constantly until the
mixture is boiling. Boil,
stirring continuously, until
soft ball stage is reached –
about 20 minutes. Take off
the heat and add the vanilla
essence. Beat until it starts to
set on the sides of the pot.
Pour into a greased tray,
leave until cold and then
score. If you find the mixture
isn't setting, bring to the boil
again for a minute or two,
then remove from the heat
and beat and that should do
the trick.

autumn

117

Hints and tips for making bread

Have all ingredients good and warm, not hot or lukewarm.

Knead, knead, knead.

When bread dough is rising keep it cosy, out of draughts and don't knock it.

Bread must be baked at a temperature of 200°C to kill the yeast.

Baked bread should be removed from tins immediately and stood on racks to cool.

An occasional feast on bread hot from the oven, dripping with butter will not harm you.

A Simple White Loaf

2 teaspoons sugar
2 teaspoons salt
500g strong white bread flour
1 sachet (7g) easy-blend yeast
1 tablespoon olive oil
300ml warm water

1   Sift the sugar, salt and flour into a large mixing bowl. Add the yeast and toss to mix. Add the oil followed by half of the water and use the handle of a wooden spoon to mix to a ball; you will need to add more water, which you should add slowly until you have a soft ball, only using the spoon handle to mix.

2   Sprinkle plenty of flour on your work surface and tip out the soft dough. Now knead the dough. Sprinkle the dough with flour and using both of your hands push down and forward with the heels of your hands and then turn the dough over. Repeat until the dough is soft and pliable and smooth. You will need to add flour as you go and you will know when the dough is ready. Form into a ball and return it to the bowl, cover with a clean cloth and set in a warm cosy spot to rise. This will take an hour or so.

3   Preheat the oven to 200°C/400°F/gas mark 6. Remove the dough from the bowl, knock down and shape to fit your buttered bread tin. Once again, set in a cosy spot to rise and when you feel it looks right bake for 35 minutes. You can also make pizzas from this dough – just make up the recipe then divide into 4 balls to make 4 pizza bases.

4   If you replace half the liquid with milk and add a few tablespoons sugar to sweeten along with a handful of dried fruit and a couple of teaspoons cinnamon and mixed spice, you have the ingredients for a fruit loaf. Replace half the flour for wholemeal flour and your will have a more nourishing loaf of bread. Instead of making up into a loaf your could shape the dough into a more rustic loaf and leave to rise on a buttered baking tray.

Oven temperature test

If your oven has no temperature gauge simply sprinkle a little flour on a baking tray, put it into the oven and wait 5 minutes. If the flour is dark brown the oven is hot enough to bake bread. If it is light brown you could bake a cake. If the flour has not turned brown, the oven is less than 140°C. If the flour is light brown, the oven is about 180°C. If the flour is dark brown, the oven is about 220°C.

Bread

A book of verse beneath the bough, a jug of wine, a loaf of bread and thou…

The staff of life.

If you have two loaves of bread, sell one and buy a lily.

Use a slice of white bread to pick up tiny fragments of glass after a breakage.

Keep bread fresh by placing a washed and dried stick of celery in the bread bin.

autumn

119

STORECUPBOARD PRESERVES AND SPICES

I make all manner of jams and jellies, and always have a couple of frozen tarts in the fridge along with a few bottles of cherries, apricots in brandy and piccalilli. I roast and grind small quantities of spices as and when I need them for cooking and store dried herbs in recycled jam jars.

Quince trees

If Eve did tempt Adam with a delicious fruit it was more than likely a quince. A golden pear-shaped fruit covered with the softest down, passionately fragrant – a single fruit will scent a room with its exotic fragrance. The perfume of quince is essentially feminine and whilst the fruit looks good enough to eat, it is hard and woody and needs first to be washed and peeled, quartered and sprinkled with sugar and a little water, then slowly roasted until it exudes a delicately fragrant nectar – utterly delicious served with softly whipped cream.

The Catalans make the most delicious cordial, while in the Middle East quinces are served as a savoury dish stuffed with mincemeat and spices.

Quince Jelly

Nothing tastes quite like my quince jelly – it is truly heavenly.

Makes 1 jar

Quarter enough quinces to fill an oven dish. Sprinkle with a little sugar and water and roast for an hour or so, or until quite soft. Remove and place in a saucepan, add water to cover and bring to the boil. Remove from the heat and push through a sieve. Measure the liquid and add a cup of granulated sugar and the juice of half a lemon. Return to the saucepan and bring to the boil. Boil until set is reached. To test for set, drop half a teaspoon of the mixture onto a chilled saucer, waiting a minute or two then nudging with your fingertip to see if it has formed a slight skin. If it has, set has been reached. If not, continue cooking for a couple of minutes then test again. Once set has been achieved, remove from the heat, pour into jars, cover and seal. This jelly is quite wonderful for breakfast on croissants or freshly buttered toast.

Fig konfyt

This is a family recipe for fig konfyt – figs preserved in rich syrup.

Makes 1 jar

Peel about 500g figs thinly removing only the outer layer. Leave overnight in a solution of 2 tablespoons bicarbonate of soda to 3 litres water. Drain. Place 800g granulated sugar, the juice of a lemon and 1 litre water in a saucepan. Bring to the boil with the peeled figs. Simmer until the fruit looks clear and full of syrup. Pack prepared jars with the fruit and cover with syrup. Seal. Eat as a conserve with croissants or as a treat on their own.

Roasting spices

Traditionally spices are stored whole to protect their flavours. Before using, spices should be toasted or roasted in a heavy-bottomed frying pan over a medium heat. This brings out the flavour of the spices. No oil or water is necessary, and you should watch over the pan as spices burn easily. Begin by heating the pan, then add the spices, berries or seeds. Allow them to sit in the pan for a couple of minutes then shake the pan about, keeping the spices moving to encourage even heating. After a few minutes a fragrance should rise and you should hear the sound of tiny pops and crackles. Remove from the pan into a grinder, I use an old pestle and mortar given to me by my mother a good 30 years ago. Once they are cool, grind away, then add the mixture to a cooking pot or store for use over the next few weeks.

Crystallised Ginger

Scrape 250g of ginger and dice roughly, taking care not to chop your fingers. Place the diced ginger in a saucepan, cover with water and stew gently until tender. Measure and add a cup of sugar for every cup of stewed ginger in water. Bring to the boil, stirring until the sugar has dissolved. Reduce the heat but continue to cook until the ginger takes on a transparent appearance. Simmer further until the syrup is greatly reduced and the ginger almost dry – you will have to watch the pan carefully as you don't want things to burn. Remove from the heat and toss the ginger in a bowl of sugar until completely covered. Leave in the sugar until quite cold then eat or store in a jar until needed.

Ginger in Syrup

Preserve ginger in large thumb-sized lumps for eating directly from the jar, or chopped small to bring a little tropical pizzazz to vanilla ice cream or to add to whipped cream and use to sandwich meringues.

250g fresh ginger
500ml water
250g granulated sugar

1 To prepare the ginger, scrape away the skin and chop into thumb-sized pieces.

2 Place the water and prepared ginger in a saucepan and bring to the boil. Simmer for 2 hours then set aside until quite cold. Ginger takes some time to soften.

3 Add the sugar to the saucepan, place over a low heat and stir until the sugar has completely dissolved. Simmer until the ginger is tender.

4 Rinse jars in boiling water then fill with the cooked ginger in syrup. Cover and seal.

Ginger for travel sickness

It is said that a journey begins with a single step. My grandmother's journeys all began when she filled a small brown paper bag with home-made crystallised ginger and tucked it into her handbag to be eaten to allay nausea during her travels.

Sip a cup of ginger tea or eat a little crystallised ginger to fend off feelings of nausea, and if you suffer from travel sickness fill a flask with ginger tea before you leave home and sip during your journey.

Peeling ginger

Don't attempt to peel ginger with a knife, rather scrape the skin off as you would scrape carrots. You will find the skin comes away easily.

Ginger in chocolate

Drain large chunks of home-preserved ginger and dip into melted dark chocolate. Place on non-stick paper to harden then transfer the chocolates into truffle cases and serve as an after-dinner treat.

Ginger and honey tea

An exotically warming drink that lifts the spirits and acts as something of a tonic.

Place a slice of ginger in a cup, fill with boiling water and allow to steep for 5 minutes. Add honey and enjoy.

A Kenyan cup of tea

Pour half milk and half water into a small saucepan. Add tea leaves to the mix and bring to the boil. Add a few slivers of ginger and sweeten to taste. Simmer for a couple of minutes and strain into cups. Serve.

autumn

Lemon and Passionfruit Curd

Makes 1 jar

1 large or 2 small passionfruit
grated rind and juice of
    2 lemons
250g sugar
150g butter
2 large eggs

Place all the ingredients in a large bowl set over a saucepan of boiling water. Stir constantly as the water bubbles below and slowly the fruity mix will turn into a fragrant custard. Pour into jars, cover and seal. Store in the fridge and enjoy spread thickly on hot wholemeal toast.

Variations

Banana Curd
4 very ripe bananas, mashed
250g sugar
150g butter
2 large eggs

Apple Curd
2 cups apple purée
250g sugar
150g butter
2 large eggs

autumn

124

Store-cupboard Apricot Chutney

Makes 4 jars

500g dried apricots
2 teaspoons garam masala
1 teaspoon curry powder
250g soft brown sugar
500ml malt vinegar
1 teaspoon grated fresh ginger (or ground ginger)
2 teaspoons salt
100g sultanas
½ teaspoon peppercorns

Soak the dried apricots overnight in 600ml water. The following day, place the soaked apricots and remaining water in a saucepan, add the other ingredients and bring to the boil, turn down the heat and simmer for 30 minutes. Pour into jars, cover and seal.

Mango Chutney

My recipe for mango chutney is cobbled together using my mother's recipe as a starting point!

Take a basket of about 3 dozen mangoes, peel and chop or mince with 110g green ginger, 50g garlic and 225g red chillies. Dissolve 290g sugar and 110g salt in 1.8 litres of good vinegar, bring to the boil and cool. Mix well with the minced ingredients and stand covered in the sun for 3–4 days, then bottle and store in the fridge. Best left for a week before eating.

Pickled Onions

Makes 4 jars

1kg pickled onions
peppercorns
bay leaves
500ml cider vinegar
2 teaspoons pickling spice
100g sugar
40g salt

Peel the onions and pack into clean prepared jars. Slip a couple of peppercorns and a bay leaf into each jar between the onions. Put the vinegar, pickling spice, sugar and salt in a saucepan and bring to the boil. Pour over the onions to fill the jars. If you like particularly hot onions, add a chilli. Seal. Store for at least 2 weeks before eating.

Home-made Chilli Sauce

Makes 1 bottle

150g fresh chillies
200g onions, peeled and chopped
1 cooking apple, peeled and chopped
1 teaspoon mustard powder
1 teaspoon sea salt
200g cider vinegar

Place all the ingredients in a saucepan and simmer gently until everything has turned into a liquidy sludge. Push through a sieve and bottle. Seal and set aside for a week before using. Beware! It is very hot.

Medlars

Medlars are hedgerow fruit, easy to grow, yet difficult to find in the wild, they are the last of the autumn fruit to be harvested. I like to imagine Elizabeth I eating medlar honey poured over bread or with curds and whey.

Medlar Jelly Sweetmeats

You need chocolate moulds to make medlar sweetmeats. The jelly can be poured into a shallow dish then cut into squares but traditionally boiled syrup is poured into moulds to set – little moulds shaped into fish, or flowers, ducks or rabbits.

Place 2kg bletted medlars in a saucepan, cover with water and bring to the boil. Simmer gently until the fruit can be mashed with a fork. Remove from the heat and strain through a sieve, pressing the pulp through as best you can (I use the back of a spoon). Measure the pulp into a clean saucepan; for every cup of pulp add a cup of sugar and a squeeze of lemon juice. If you wish, add a pinch of allspice too. Bring to the boil, stirring constantly, then boil until a good setting point is reached. Spoon into wet moulds and set aside until firm.

Medlar Honey

Medlars are ripe for cooking when the flesh has rotted somewhat. When the flesh is soft and brown the flavour is full.

Makes 1–2 jars

2kg medlars
1 kg granulated sugar

Quarter the medlars and place in a large saucepan. Cover with a litre of water. Bring to the boil. Simmer gently until the medlars are soft enough to mash. Remove from the heat and set aside to cool. Strain through a sieve lined with muslin, squeezing out well to get every drop of the liquid. Pour into a large saucepan and add a cup of sugar for each cup of liquid. Bring slowly to the boil stirring constantly. Boil for about half an hour, then drop a small spoonful into a glass of iced water – if it holds together it is ready. Pour into prepared bottles and seal. Store in the fridge.

Medlar Jelly

Medlar jelly sets with ease, so add a little more water than usual when making a jelly to spread on toast or scones.

Makes 1–2 jars

2kg bletted medlars
500ml water
juice of ½ lemon

Place the fruit in a saucepan and cover with the water. Simmer until soft and mushy then strain through muslin. Measure the juice and place in a saucepan. Add a cup of sugar for every cup of juice. Add the lemon juice and bring to the boil, stirring constantly. Boil for about 20 minutes watching carefully, then check for set (*see p.120*). If it is ready, remove from the heat and pour into prepared jam jars, cover and seal.

Autumn puffballs

You need just the right conditions (and a good book for identifying them!) to find edible wild mushrooms – a warmish, dampish autumn. Puffballs are easy to spot, white football-sized orbs sitting in the grass. Only harvest healthy looking specimens. Eat slices fried in olive oil with fried eggs and tomatoes, or cube and add to risottos.

How to dry mushrooms

If you have plenty of interesting mushrooms about it is an idea to dry some. To do this thread mushrooms onto a string and hang above a kitchen range (or dry in a low oven). When quite dry store in a glass jar. They make a good addition to winter soups and stews.

Mushroom Ketchup

Makes 1 litre

2kg large open mushrooms, sliced
50g salt
1 onion, sliced
600ml wine vinegar
1 teaspoon ground allspice
good pinch of mace
1cm fresh ginger, finely chopped

Place the mushrooms in a bowl, cover and refrigerate for 2 days. Tip into a saucepan and add the other ingredients. Bring to the boil and simmer gently for half an hour. Strain, bottle, seal and store in the fridge or freeze in suitable containers.

THE AUTUMN GARDEN

Scrub flower pots in preparation for spring and generally tidy the garden. If you have any broken pots, place them strategically around the garden, half burying them and leaving an opening for frogs and toads to hide.

Ladybird houses

Cut hollow bamboo into 15cm lengths, lash together with string and wedge in dry corners of the garden for ladybirds and other bugs to hide in during the winter months.

Bird boxes

Clean bird boxes and feeders in readiness for spring. Wearing gloves, remove all nesting materials from boxes, give them a wash in warm water to which you have added a little vinegar and some soap flakes. Wash bird feeders in the same way.

Build a compost heap

A compost heap needs to be at least a metre square to function properly. The greenery and kitchen scraps are heated to a level where bacteria and earthworms turn it into wonderful sweet-smelling nutritious compost. Choose a spot in the garden that is easily accessible and not in full view of the house; if you have a vegetable garden the compost heap could sit to one side. As you can imagine the soil around the compost heap becomes very rich. I plant a mixture of something pretty like nasturtiums and alkanet with something useful like comfrey and a couple of pumpkin seeds there.

Prepare bulbs for indoor winter flowering

Early autumn is the time of year for potting up spring bulbs in preparation for winter flowering. Tulips, narcissus, hyacinths, crocus, grape hyacinths and lily of the valley can all be prepared in this way. Purchase healthy bulbs early in the season, place them in a brown paper bag and store in the vegetable section of your refrigerator for 12 weeks – a temperature of 1.7–8.9°C is best. This tricks the bulb into thinking winter has set in and once removed they respond as if it is spring. Plant into pots with good potting compost. Bulbs should be settled gently into the compost, the tips standing above the surface of the soil. Water well and place in a warm spot, ideally 10–15°C. Do not allow the soil to dry out. Once leaves have begun to form, pots should be positioned in the home, in good warm, light situations. Bulbs take on average 10 weeks from planting to flowering, so bear this in mind.

Faggots and fir cones

Harvest twigs, fir cones and sticks during crunchy autumn walks. Break up and tie twigs and sticks in small bundles with string and store in a dry shed along with fir cones for winter use. Place in a basket beside the fireplace ready to use as firelighters.

Autumn garden tips and tasks

When using a bulb planter, don't try and remove the plug of earth it pulls by hand, it will be forced out when you make the second hole.

Plant rhubarb crowns and divide old plants.

Tidy the garden, clean out the pond.

Harvest pumpkins and squash.

Buy autumn flowering cyclamen and plant out.

An arrangement of colourful autumn leaves in a large vase will bring a little autumn glory into your home.

Prune rambling and climbing roses, cutting away any untidy shoots right down to the base and tying up new shoots. Cut away side shoots that spoil the shape of climbers. I usually push a few of the prunings into my cuttings row in the vegetable garden (optimistically, as they don't always take!).

autumn

129

HOME REMEDIES

Our grandmothers relied heavily on homemade remedies. With a mixture of herbs and traditional wisdom they nursed their families through winter coughs and colds. A diet rich in fresh fruit and vegetables, good basic hygiene and a warm home helped fight off infection before it took hold.

Lip Balm

2 tablespoons almond oil
1 teaspoon beeswax
1 vitamin E capsule

Melt all the ingredients together over a low heat, then pour into a small tub and leave to set. Apply to protect your lips against the cold north wind.

A soupy remedy for worms

Wash and chop a whole butternut squash. Place in a saucepan and cover with water. Bring to the boil and simmer until soft. Remove from the heat. Put the entire cooked squash, pips, skin, cooking water and all in blender. Blend until quite smooth. Add salt and pepper and a little stock if you need to thin it a little. Have a bowl of this soup every day for a week and your body will expel the worms. This is another traditional South African remedy.

Honey and Thyme Cough Mixture

Place a sprig of freshly picked thyme in a saucepan, add a cup of water and bring to the boil. Remove from the heat and set aside to cool. Strain into a fresh cup and sweeten with honey. Sip through the day to relieve a tickly cough.

Elderberry Rob

Take daily as a tonic, or occasionally to relieve the symptoms of colds, coughs, flu and chesty infections.

Harvest ripe elderberries in late summer or early autumn. Rinse in clean water, picking through and discarding any split or rotting berries. Place in a saucepan, cover with water and bring to the boil. Simmer gently with the lid on for about 30 minutes, adding more water to keep the fruit covered. Cool and mash with a potato masher.

Strain through muslin, squeezing as much juice as you can from the fruit. Measure the liquid into a clean saucepan and for every cup of juice add one cup of sugar. Bring slowly to the boil, stirring constantly with a wooden spoon to dissolve the sugar. Boil for 5 minutes then remove from the heat and pour into clean bottles and seal.

Elderberry Rob has a strong hedgerow flavour – take a tablespoon or so in a cup with boiling water.

Elderberry Rob can also be used as cassis – add a flavoursome teaspoon or so to white wine.

Onion and Honey Cough Syrup

A South African remedy

Chop an onion, place in a bowl and cover with honey and allow to sit in the fridge. After 24 hours take a teaspoon of the liquid as a cough mixture. Many people swear by this remedy.

Winter health tips

An apple a day keeps the doctor away.

Try taking a teaspoon of good local honey through the winter to lessen the effects of spring hayfever.

Sprinkle a few drops of olbas oil on your pillow to ease a sniffle.

Mustard Foot Bath

To improve circulation and eliminate headaches.

Place 2 tablespoons mustard seeds in a pestle and mortar, pound roughly and add to a bowl of hot water. When the temperature is comfortable, place you feet in the water and sit back and relax. As the water cools remove your feet, dry and relax for a further 20 minutes.

Garlic for good health

Eat plenty of garlic during the cold months – it improves circulation and helps kill all those cold bugs floating about.

autumn

Eucalyptus gargle

Place 3 or 4 eucalyptus leaves in 250ml boiling water, set aside for 10 minutes. Strain into a cup. Use as a gargle for sore throats and mouth ulcers.

Burn a porcupine quill to cure a nosebleed

In Zimbabwe nosebleeds are cured with the smoke from a burning porcupine quill. The quill is lit and held at waist level and the patient takes a breath of the gently spiralling smoke through his nose. The nosebleed stops almost immediately.

Lemon and honey ice lollies

Suitable for adults and children suffering from minor colds and sore throats. When I kept bees I would make up lemon and honey ice lollies and keep them in the freezer, serving them up as and when needed. I would recommend using New Zealand Manuka honey as this has been found to contain many healing properties. I often add about 20 drops of echinacea tincture to the mixture to increase the healing properties.

Makes 6 lollies

Take the juice of 2 lemons, stir into 2 cups of warm water and add half a cup of Manuka honey. Stir to dissolve the honey. Pour into ice lolly moulds and freeze.

Ginger bath

For stiffness in the joints and rheumatic pain.

Put a chunk of ginger, thinly sliced, in 1 litre water, bring to the boil and then simmer for 15 minutes before adding to a bath.

Cabbage leaves

For nursing mothers.

Cupping nursing breasts with bruised cabbage leaves relieves sore nipples, improves the flow of milk, and relieves the discomfort of mastitis and menstrual breast pain. Crush conveniently shaped, fresh cabbage leaves with your hands then hold in place by tucking inside your bra.

Fennel seed infusion

To soothe tired eyes.

Soak half a teaspoon of fennel seeds in 125ml boiling water for 5 minutes. Strain and set aside to cool. Dip 2 cotton wool pads in the cooled infusion, squeeze out any excess then place a pad on each eye; lie back and relax for 10 minutes.

Lemon balm tea

Place a few lemon balm leaves in a cup of boiling water. Sip to relieve a feverish cold.

WINTER

The aroma of pine needles, the jingling of bells, warm log fires and scrabble, pots of tea, deep red wine, gilded fruit and nuts, thick slabs of fruit cake. The ancients celebrated midwinter; it has always been a time of feasting and in these modern times we walk in their footsteps, celebrating Christmas and New Year, feasting on what were once, for most, unimaginable luxuries, but through all this traditions continue and the concept of family, large or small, still sits at the heart of every home.

MIDWINTER IN THE GARDEN

Once the land was full of indigenous plants, a feast for the birds, nowadays gardens are planted with exotics, which don't always provide food for the birds. You can hang out bird feeders, lard balls and crumbs in full view of the house, and keep a count of varieties of feathered friends.

Midwinter bird feast

Make a small hole in an empty, well-washed yogurt pot. Thread a loop of twine down through the hole. The bird cake will be suspended from this loop.

Place wholemeal breadcrumbs, sunflower seeds, unsalted crushed nuts, raisins and grated apple in a bowl. Pour melted lard over the mixture and mix to form a gloppy dough that holds together well. Pour into the yogurt pot and leave to set. You might want to make a few of them. To use, cut and tear away the yogurt pot and hang the bird cake from a branch away from the reach of cats and where you can watch it from inside the house.

Thread peanuts onto a long length of string and use to decorate a tree in the garden. Keep the peanuts company with a few yogurt pot bird cakes and watch the birds feasting.

Cleaning tools

Use a wire brush and steel wool to scrub away any rust on tools or furniture and buff up with an oily cloth.

Lightly sand any wooden handles and wipe both metal and wood surfaces with linseed oil.

Icy outdoor baubles

When winter sets in and the land is frozen, fill shallow bowls with water, sprinkle red rosehips, colourful dried autumn leaves and any seed pods or twigs and leave outside to freeze solid then shake out. Use a very hot knitting needle to make a hole in each one and loop binder twine or string and hang your icy baubles from the branches of a tree. They will last until the weather changes.

POTPOURRI

When I first came to live in England I fell in love with the pretty cottage gardens, full of buzzing bees and fragrant flowers and herbs, blue tits and robins. I planted my first English garden full of all manner of sweet-smelling things, with the most romantic of names: auriculas, bachelor's buttons, spicy pinks, heart's ease, cowslips, primulas, clary and pineapple sage to name but a few.

Use a knitting needle to prick a pattern of holes in a fresh orange. Press a clove in each hole and roll the stuck orange in a little ground orris root to assist preservation. Tie the prepared orange with ribbon and hang somewhere dark and airy for a few months. In time the orange will dry but the fragrance will linger for many months.

The idea that I could dry these flowers and leaves to hold their fragrance and mix them into potpourri fascinated me. Through that first summer I had bunches of lavender and rosebuds hanging from the beams in the kitchen along with poppy heads which rained down a noisy harvest of seeds one warm autumn evening, and masses of petals drying on racks made of muslin nailed to stick frames in the shed.

Through the first winter I mixed dried leaves and petals, buds and spices with orris root and fragrant wood chips to create potpourris full of the fragrance of summer. I filled muslin and velvet bags of the stuff, tied them with ribbon and sold dozens of them at the local craft markets.

If you intend drying your own leaves and petals you will need a drying frame of sorts. Any frame will do – nail wire mesh or muslin across it to hold the drying bounty in thin layers. Place in a very dry spot where the air is moving and there is no chance of damp. When the leaves and petals are quite dry, place in large screw-top jars. I have a bowl of dried red roses, petals and buds, saved from the summer, fragrant with spices and rose oil, set on my dressing table.

Citrus Potpourri

1 cup dried orange peel

2 cups dried lemon verbena
  leaves

2 cups dried yellow rose
  petals

2 cups dried calendula petals

1 tablespoon ground orris
  root

2 teaspoons ground cinnamon

½ cup cinnamon sticks

Christmas Potpourri

4 cups dried rose petals

1 cup dried orange peel

1 cup eucalyptus leaves

1 cup cinnamon sticks

2 tablespoons dried cloves

6 drops cinnamon essential oil

6 drops bergamot essential oil

2 tablespoons ground orris
  root

Perfume Powder

Grind together 25g each of
cloves, nutmeg, cinnamon,
caraway seed and tonka beans
and add 150g ground orris
root. This spicy powder can be
added to potpourri or placed
in small muslin bags to be
slipped between clean
clothing.

Home-made blankets

In the corner of my study I
have what I call my blanket
basket. In it I save balls of
double knitting wool picked
up for very little at charity
shops or bought from sale
baskets in yarn shops.
Occasionally a friend will
bring over a couple of half
balls left over from a project
or I unravel a jumper, winding
and washing the wool, then
rolling it into balls and into
the basket it will go.
Eventually I knit the blanket.
I generally choose a simple
style, knitting or crocheting
squares. I cast on 40 stitches
and knit 40 rows, either in
one colour or multicoloured
squares. When I start knitting
a blanket I usually have a
design in mind and I love the
sense of achievement when I
sew the last square into place.

DARK DAYS

One needs to prepare for the dark days of winter. I keep a few hidden treats – special ginger and chocolate oat biscuits, a fruit cake and in the freezer packets of raspberries saved from the summer, ready to be brought out on special days.

Rag rugs

Rug-making equipment is minimal. A hook, which can often be bought for pennies from a charity shop, and new costs but little; plenty of fabric strips, torn from leftover clothes and old linen; hessian, which sells for next to nothing, to hook through; a little imagination and time, and of course a basket to store it all in.

Making a rag rug is an exercise in thrift. First you have to collect the fabric. You can scour jumble sales for old shirts and used-up summer dresses and combine these with what you find going through your rag bag and exhausted bed linen. When you have a good pile of cloth it will need to be torn into 4cm wide strips and folded, pattern side outwards, before being rolled into manageable balls or yarn.

Before you start, be sure to practise hooking the fabric strips. Work evenly, keeping the loops the same size and close together to create a smooth surface. It's an idea to visit your local textile museum to have a look at the real thing, then set to. Start the design process one rainy January day by drawing with a permanent marker on a large piece of hessian cloth, then hooking can commence. You will enjoy many hours spent rug-hook-in-hand, poking and looping the prepared yarn tightly through the hessian.

Firewood

Find a good woodman and talk to him, let him know what you will be doing with wood he delivers. Henry Streatfield was my woodman for 15 years. A lovely man, he had a good turn of phrase and would deliver the wood, then with a child on my knee, we would assertively put the world to rights with our polarised views on life.

Do you burn wood to keep warm or do you cook on it? Do you prefer to keep the fire going overnight or is it an occasional thing, you know, roaring fire on a rainy Saturday afternoon, rugby on the telly, jigsaw on the table, Stilton and crackers, a fruit cake and a glass of something or a tray of tea. However you use wood it is worth telling the woodman. If he is worth his salt he will supply you with just the right stuff. My woodman would leave me hardwoods for a long slow burn, apple and oak for rainy Saturday log fires and small softwood logs, sometimes even willow for starting the fire or burning quick and hot in the range or wood burner. Occasionally, Henry would even leave a few large logs for me to split when things were getting me down!

MEND AND MAKE DO

Once everyone had a mending basket. Pleasurable hours would be spent neatly stitching together rips or darning holes. A mending basket is a must in my home. In it I keep needles and thread, a selection of buttons and some iron-on lining.

Mending

Place items for mending in a basket and enjoy regular sessions replacing buttons, sewing up hems or completing any other minor repairs. Care for the clothes you love to wear and they will last and last.

Vintage and recycle

The fashion for vintage clothing means extra care for old fabrics, fine laces or linens. Often a new set of buttons or edging will give new life to a garment.

Handbags and purses

Regularly, go through all your handbags and purses, shake out and dust, sponge away any stains or marks. Inspect each item closely. Clean handbag mirrors with a soft cloth and a little vinegar solution. Clean away any marks then use a little olive oil on a soft cloth to wipe over leather bags. Polish metal buckles and put away ready for use.

Shoes

Always store good shoes in their boxes. If shoes get wet, dry them away from direct heat. Stuff with scrunched newspaper to keep in shape.

If shoes need re-heeling take them to your local shoe repair shop.

To keep shoes sweet-smelling place small cotton bags containing bicarbonate of soda in shoes between wearings. Bicarb sprinkled in shoes and left overnight will remove bad smells.

Espadrilles will resist the dirt for much longer if sprayed with starch before you wear them.

Clean shoes after wearing.

Patent leather shoes and bags: Wipe with a damp cloth to remove any dust and dirt, wipe dry then buff with a little petroleum jelly spread on a soft cloth.

Canvas and cloth shoes: Brush lightly with a soft bristle brush then sponge away any marks.

Clean leather shoes with the appropriate leather cleaners, buffing up to a good shine.

Scuffed leather shoes should be rubbed with a piece of raw potato before polishing.

Roughen the soles of slippery shoes with sandpaper.

ALL ABOUT BATTER

Batter puddings are a very British tradition, every county has a traditional recipe to be proud of, sweetened with sugar or fruit or savoury to eat with gravy, but the batter remains the same, sometimes enriched with cream or melted butter, others eked out with watered down milk.

Properly discovering batter was a revelation to me. Yes, I had always made pancakes but never considered it batter. When my eldest daughter Zolii was 16 and at catering college she let me into a secret. I'd never been terribly good at making Yorkshire puddings; I persevered but they were never as light, as crisp or as good as I wanted. All of this changed in a single phone call. And this is what she told me: 'Mum, it's simple. Use half water and half milk to make it, and it should be the consistency of pouring cream. Allow the mixed batter to stand at room temperature for half an hour before using it. Make sure the batter pans are well oiled, not buttered. They should have sufficient oil in them to move when tipped. Preheat the pans until the oil is smoking hot. When the batter pours into the pans it should immediately begin to cook. Toad in the Hole, Yorkshire puddings, pancakes, Kent Cherry Pudding, Apple Batter Pudding – all made with batter, and more or less the same batter!'

Batter Mix

Whisk together 150ml milk and 150ml water, 2 eggs, 125g plain flour and a good pinch of salt. When the batter is quite smooth set aside for 20 minutes to settle.

Individual Yorkshire Puddings

This quantity of batter makes a single Yorkshire pudding in a tin measuring 20 × 30cm or 18 small puddings. I prefer individual portions.

Make up the batter. Pour oil into each of the dishes in a muffin or fairy cake pan and heat on the top rack in a hot oven. When the oil is smoking remove the pan and pour batter mix into each case. Bake in the middle of a hot oven for 20–25 minutes, allowing space for the batter to rise. Serve immediately with plenty of good gravy and roast beef, roast chicken, nut roast, roast vegetables, roast pork – in fact roast everything!

As a boy, my father's mother served freshly baked, crisp batter pudding smothered in golden syrup as a fill-you-up treat to her children.

Toad in the Hole with Onion Gravy

Serves 2

1 Make up the batter (*see left*).

2 Preheat the oven to 190°C/375°F/gas mark 5.

3 Place 6 good sausages in a 20 × 30cm roasting tin along with 4 tablespoons olive or sunflower oil and cook in the oven for 15 minutes. Turn up the heat to 200°C/400°F/gas mark 6 for 5 minutes and, very quickly, remove the roasting tin from the oven, take out the sausages and put them on a plate for a minute. Pour the batter into the smoking oil, and replace the sausage strategically in the already cooking batter. Return to the oven and bake for about 25 minutes. After 15 minutes turn the heat down to 180°C/350°F/gas mark 4. Serve with mashed potatoes and Onion Gravy.

Onion Gravy

Fry a large peeled and sliced onion in a couple of tablespoons of oil. Remove the onions. Add a rounded tablespoon of plain flour to the pan along with enough oil to make a smooth paste. Cook for a minute or two then add 250ml vegetable or beef stock and a few drops of soy sauce. Stir or whisk until the mixture is bubbling and gravy-like. Return the onion rings and stir well. Serve in a warm jug or simply pour over the plated up Toad in the Hole.

Apple Batter Pudding

Preheat the oven to 200°C/400°F/gas mark 6. Whisk together 150ml milk and 150ml water, 3 tablespoons sugar, 2 eggs, 125g plain flour and a good pinch of salt. Peel and chop 500g cooking apples, sprinkle with sugar and cinnamon and bake for 10–15 minutes to cook the apples. Remove from the oven, add 3 tablespoons melted butter to the batter then pour it over the cooked apples. Return to the oven and bake for 15 minutes at 200°C and 10 minutes at 180°C/350°F/gas mark 4. Sprinkle with sugar and serve immediately.

Kent Cherry Pudding

Preheat the oven to 200°C/400°F/gas mark 6. Make up the batter (*see p.144*). Add 3 tablespoons caster sugar and 25g melted butter, whisk together then add a large handful of stoned cherries, stir and pour into a preheated baking dish containing 50g very hot melted butter. Bake for 15 minutes at 200°C and 10 minutes at 180°C/350°F/gas mark 4. Sprinkle with sugar and serve immediately. It is delicious piping hot with a spoonful of cherries in brandy or cherries in syrup. This pudding does not keep.

winter

WINTER DRINKS

In days gone by, before we all had central heating, a hot drink enjoyed beside a glowing fire would warm inside and out. My children loved hot apple juice when they were little, made with apple juice and boiling water. Wassail is the traditional English county drink – a perfect winter warmer.

Mulled Wine

2 bottles red wine
1 apple stuck with 6 cloves
1 orange, sliced
2 cinnamon sticks
1 bottle apple juice

Mix all together in a saucepan and heat gently over a low flame.

Mulling White Wine

Hot white wine flavoured with pears is just a little different. I love it.

1 bottle Pinot Grigio,
1 litre pear and grape juice
2 cinnamon sticks
a sliced lemon stuck with 4 cloves
a handful of pear crisps

Mix all together in a saucepan and heat gently over a low flame.

Wassail

Wassailing means different things to different people. In the village my children grew up in, wassailing meant carol singing, walking warmly dressed between the scattered houses, along frosty lanes, standing at the doors singing, often being welcomed in for a glass of something – occasionally a glass of wassail. Wassail to others is New Year's Eve, celebrations and bonfires, times to share and bring cheer, to bless the apple trees, to remind the good Earth that soon the days will lengthen and spring will come.

Sufficient for 10 people
500g crab or cooking apples
½ teaspoon grated nutmeg
small piece of bruised ginger
3 cloves
2 cinnamon sticks
100g sugar
4 litres cider
brandy if you are brave

Simmer the apples, spices and sugar in a little water until the apples are soft. Add the cider and heat slowly, not allowing the mixture to boil. Strain into a serving bowl and add a good splash of brandy. Serve in mugs or punch cups.

MIDWINTER FEASTING

Every family has their traditional Christmas dinner – when the children were little we had turkey, but our move to Suffolk meant pheasant reigned supreme, along with an almond and sage nut roast. I stuff the birds with a mixture of apples and onion.

The festive roast goose

Each Christmas throughout my childhood we had turkey on the table. My father was always slightly scornful of this habit, and would tell us stories from his childhood. Born in 1902 in the city of York, he would tell us seasonal tales of narrow cobbled streets with shop frontages hanging with freshly plucked geese – of course there were turkeys but evidently a goose was the wise housewife's choice. Not only would a family enjoy mouth-watering slices of roast goose and the crispest roast potatoes and flavoursome gravy but there was also the goose fat to be made into salves and creams and, horror of horror, to be rubbed on your chest to keep you warm through the icy winters!

In Britain goose is traditionally stuffed with sage and onion and served with gravy and apple sauce. In Russia it is stuffed with seasoned shredded cabbage and onions. In Scandinavia it is rubbed with lemon and stuffed with chopped cooking apples, onions and prunes which are often removed before serving to be made up into a sauce served alongside the roast bird. In Germany roast goose is served with boiled potatoes and sauerkraut at Christmas.

Vivienne's roast goose

Preheat the oven to 190°C/375°F/gas mark 5. Rub the goose inside and out with lemon juice. Stuff with a mixture of freshly chopped sage, onion, breadcrumbs, parsley and grated apple, well seasoned and bound with an egg. Place the goose in a roasting pan with a little water, cover the breast with a little foil to prevent it from burning and place in the oven. Half an hour into the cooking time remove from the oven and prick the bird well to relieve the fat. Spread the breast with a little honey and return to the oven. Continue to cook. Allow 30 minutes for every 500g weight of the bird. When cooked, check to ensure the goose is cooked through by pricking the area between breast and thigh – the juices should run clear. Remove from the roasting pan to a rack for the fat to drain. Save all goose fat for future use – to roast potatoes or make salves, or possibly to wrap your children with goose grease and brown paper against winter chills!

How to tell your goose is cooked

Remove from the heat. Take a fork and prick between the thigh and body. If the juices run clear the bird is cooked; if pink your bird should be returned to the oven for further cooking.

Gilded Poussin on jewelled rice

Serves 2

2 poussins
50g butter
2 tablespoons boiling water
1 teaspoon saffron
1 egg yolk
ground sea salt and black pepper
150g basmati rice
pinch of saffron
2 tablespoons currants
2 tablespoons each red, yellow and
    green peppers, chopped

Preheat the oven to 220°C/425°F/gas mark 7.

Butter the poussins outside and in and place uncovered in a hot oven.

Pour the boiling water into a small bowl, add the saffron and allow it to soak for 5 minutes before whisking in the egg yolk.

After 15 minutes remove the poussins from the oven and paint on the saffron and egg mixture. Return to the oven. Repeat twice during the cooking period.

The birds should be roasted for about 30 minutes altogether, or until cooked.

To make the jewelled rice, prepare basmati rice for two, adding the saffron to the cooking water. Once cooked, toss in a splash of olive oil, and add the currants and chopped red, green and yellow peppers.

How to make gravlax at home

Serves about 8

50g sea salt
25g caster sugar
20ml wholegrain mustard
25g ground black peppercorns
10g ground allspice
50ml gin
bunch of dill leaves, chopped
1kg salmon fillet, preferably one side skin removed
olive oil

Measure the salt, sugar, mustard, pepper, allspice and gin into a bowl and mix to a paste, add most of the dill and mix further. Line a large platter with good quality clingfilm, spread with half the paste and lay the salmon on top of the paste. Spread the remaining paste over the upper side of the salmon to completely cover the fish. Fold the clingfilm over the fish, encasing it, and wrap with a second layer of clingfilm. Place in the fridge for 24 hours. Remove, wash under cold running water and pat dry. Rub with olive oil and sprinkle with the remaining dill. Serve with dill sauce. Will keep wrapped in clingfilm in the fridge for 5 days.

Dill Sauce

In a small bowl place 30g caster sugar, 1 teaspoon salt, 30ml white wine vinegar and 30ml Dijon mustard. Use a whisk to mix thoroughly then add 125ml olive oil. Whisk until you have a smooth sauce, then stir in 2 tablespoons freshly chopped dill and serve with thinly sliced gravlax.

Fresh Horseradish Sauce

This wonderfully British plant can be found growing wild in ditches and on banks around the country. The root is large and can be woody. To grow your own horseradish, plant root cuttings or obtain small plants from a specialist nursery. Set in rich soil and wait. In time the plant will flourish and every now and again you will be able to harvest some root, grate it and add it to a little fresh cream, season with salt and a little sugar to serve with roast beef or to enjoy spread thinly on sliced tomato sandwiches.

Roasting times:

For well done: 25 minutes per 500g at 200°C/400°F/gas mark 6

For medium: 20 minutes per 500g at 200°C/400°F/gas mark 6

For rare: 15 minutes per 500g at 200°C/400°F/gas mark 6

Roast Rib of Beef served with Horseradish Sauce

A rib of beef was central to the old English midwinter feast. Midwinter was a time when fresh food was scarce. The slaughter of such a large beast meant a time of feasting for all. Vegetables were roasted or boiled and pottages of barley, oats and dried beans would be cooked. Bread would be on the tables to soak up the meat juices and gravies.

2.5kg rib of beef
1 teaspoon each of sea salt and black pepper
beef stock
plain flour
half a wine glass of port or red wine
½ teaspoon wholegrain mustard
300ml beef or vegetable stock

1　Preheat the oven to 220°C/425°F/gas mark 7.

2　Splash a little olive oil into a roasting pan and place in the oven to heat. Season the meat with sea salt and black pepper. Remove the pan from the oven and set the beef in the centre of it. Roast for 20 minutes to seal the meat, then turn down the heat to 200°C/400°F/gas mark 6 and cook to your preference (*see below*).

3　When the cooking time is up, remove from the oven. Transfer the beef to a carving board or serving plate to rest for 20 minutes before carving. (If your kitchen is not very warm cover the meat loosely with foil and a folded tea towel to hold the warmth.)

4　Place the roasting tin over a moderate heat and sprinkle with a little flour then, using a wooden spoon, scrape away at the base of the tin, while mixing the flour and the fat to create a roux. Add the port, mustard and 300ml good beef or vegetable stock. Bring to a simmer then strain through a sieve into a warmed jug or gravy boat. After carving be sure to stir any juices into the gravy.

Roast Winter Vegetables

Peel potatoes, butternut squash, onions, carrots, celeriac and parsnips. Cut to a similar size. Place all but the squash and the onions in a saucepan covered with cold water and bring to the boil, simmer for 3 minutes then drain and toss in olive oil. Splash some olive oil in a roasting tin and place in a hot oven. When the oil is piping hot add all the prepared vegetables, sprinkle liberally with salt and rosemary and roast until crisp and golden brown.

Tips

Save water from cooking vegetables to water your houseplants. It is full of nutrients that should not be poured down the waste pipe.

To keep Jerusalem artichokes from turning black when they are cooked, simply scrub and boil in their skins, which will easily peel off once cooked.

CHRISTMAS DECORATIONS

Putting up the decorations should be a jolly family affair, full of pomp and ceremony. The children and I always put the decorations up together though I must admit to moving things around on the tree to satisfy both my mother's pride and my designer's eye!

Pomegranates and paper chains

When they were growing up, my children always made paper chains, miles of them and we would pin them up around the rooms, along the beams, decorating corners with paper bells and holly. The Christmas tree was always as tall as possible and decorated with a mix of carefully chosen blown-glass baubles collected over the years, and my home-crafted decorations, little embroidered felt stockings, real Victorian scraps made festive with golden borders and little gilded poppy pods, tied with golden bows and wire loops attached to remind us of nature's bounty.

A laurel wreath

Wouldn't you just love someone to give you a gilded bay laurel wreath – it could hang in the kitchen to be used leaf by leaf in milk puddings and to flavour stews.

If you have a bay tree, pick sprigs and make up into a laurel wreath, gild a few of the leaves and place in a tissue-lined gift box.

Gilded poppy pods

You need to sow opium poppy seeds in the spring; they germinate easily in most soils, but prefer a sunny spot. By summer the plants will be standing tall and covered with colour paper petalled flowers, which attract hoverflies and other useful bugs. I always save seed separately from the darkest flowers, hoping for an almost black blossom the following year!

Harvest the poppy pods after flowering and hang upside down in bunches of 4 or 5 to dry. Keep watch though – when the conditions are right the pods will release millions of tiny black seeds. You should save these: some to sow anywhere you think needs a splash of summer colour, and the rest to use in seed cakes or sprinkled over bread dough before baking.

Once you have your dried poppy pods, turn them upside down and trim off the stalks, push little wire loops into the tops and glue in place with a glue gun or a blob of white glue. Set aside to dry, then paint with gold acrylic paint and while still tacky sprinkle with the finest gold glitter. When they are quite dry tie little ribbon bows beneath the loops. I store them wrapped in gold tissue and construct little boxes from heavy watercolour paper to keep them safe between Christmases.

Gilding a pomegranate

Gilding is an honourable and ancient art. Gilded pomegranates decorated feasting tables in Tudor times. Gold leaf can be easily purchased from art shops. If the fruit or nuts are to be eaten, do buy culinary gold leaf from a cake decorating shop or online and follow the simple directions. (You can use the same gold leaf to decorate home-made chocolates).

**gold leaf
size
a brush for painting on the size
a brush for applying the leaf
a soft cloth fur burnishing**

Wipe the fruit with a damp cloth. This will remove any dust or dirt.

Paint size on the fruit. To produce a mottled look, allowing the natural colours of the pomegranate skin to be displayed, only apply the size in areas you want the gold leaf to stick. Set aside until the size is tacky to the touch.

Lift a single sheet of gold leaf and lay over the fruit. Use a paintbrush to gently press the leaf to the size. Burnish the leaf covered areas with a soft cloth.

winter

153

CHRISTMAS TREATS

Homemade from your kitchen a jar of fruit mince wrapped in jolly Christmas wrapping complete with a sprig of holly will bring pleasure to both you and the recipient. I always make chocolates, carefully placed in a small gift box and wrapped in star-spangled tissue paper.

My Bûche de Noël (Chocolate Log)

Serves 8

50g caster sugar
5 egg yolks
100g dark chocolate, melted
½ teaspoon vanilla extract
4 egg whites
pinch of cream of tartar
30g sugar
cocoa powder

Filling
250ml double cream
3 tablespoons dulce de leche
6 tablespoons chestnut purée

1 Preheat the oven to 180°C/350°F/gas mark 4.

2 Line a swiss roll tin or any 40 × 30cm baking tin with baking parchment or buttered greaseproof paper.

3 Whisk the caster sugar with the egg yolks until the beaters leave a trail. Add the melted dark chocolate and vanilla extract. Mix. In a second bowl whisk the egg whites and cream of tartar until soft peaks form. Add the sugar and mix until quite stiff.

4 Fold the egg white mixture into the egg yolk mixture and pour into the prepared baking tin.

5 Bake for 15 minutes then test with a cocktail stick. If the cocktail stick comes out clean the cake is cooked. If not cook for a further 3 minutes. Remove from the oven and lay a clean tea-towel over the top of the cake while still in the tin. Tip out onto the work surface. Taking hold of one end of the teatowel roll the warm cake into a loose Swiss roll shape. Set aside to cool.

6 When cool unroll the cake. Whip the double cream and fold in the dulce de leche and chestnut purée and then spread a thick layer over the cake, reserving a little for the top. Reform the cake, rolling into shape and setting down on the serving plate with the join at the base. Spread a little of the cream filling over the top of the cake, sprinkle with cocoa powder and place chocolate holly leaves decoratively to one side. Serve with afternoon tea.

Chocolates that fizzle

How to make truffles that fizzle in your mouth as your eat them. This is an Enid Blyton hangover!

Measure 225g good plain chocolate along with 140ml double cream in a metal bowl set over a saucepan of simmering water. When completely melted, remove from the heat and whisk with an electric whisk until nearly doubled in size. When almost set stir in 4 tablespoons Space Dust. Place in the fridge to set, which should only take about half an hour. Use a melon baller to scoop and shape chocolate balls. Roll the balls in cocoa powder and your truffles are ready to eat. The 'fizzle' doesn't last long so eat within a day or two.

Edna's Bourbon Balls

My cousin Peta Gale lives in one of those dream clapboard houses set in a Maryland farming community. Peta gave me this recipe, which was given to her by Edna, her neighbour. Peta makes these to enjoy each Christmas and Thanksgiving.

150g dark chocolate
3 tablespoons golden syrup
½ cup bourbon
2½ cups vanilla wafer crumbs
½ cup sifted icing sugar
1 cup finely chopped nuts

Break the chocolate into a bowl and set to melt over a saucepan of boiling water. Once melted, add the golden syrup and the bourbon. Stir to mix then add everything else. Set aside for a few minutes to settle and cool slightly. Shape into small balls about the size of large marbles. Allow to mature for a day or two before eating.

Blazing Apples

One of our family traditions is to end a festive meal with a dish of roast apples, brought to the table flaming dramatically to be set down before the youngest person who gets to portion up and pass around the pudding.

Core enough bramley apples for everyone, stuff with fruit mince and bake dotted with butter in a medium oven for about half an hour. To serve, transfer into a serving dish. Heat a few tablespoons of brandy in a saucepan and, just before carrying the dish through, set the brandy alight and pour it over the cooked apples.

Snap dragon

I'm not sure that I should be writing this, however....This somewhat dangerous parlour game consists of tossing raisins on a platter of burning brandy. The aim is to see how many raisins you can lift from the flames without burning your fingers. It didn't seem to do us much harm!

Lavender Creams

This recipe is a favourite of mine, an adult take on peppermint creams. I shape them with a tiny flower cutter used to shape icing, and decorate them with tiny dots of yellow icing. Eaten from a tissue-lined box they are heavenly.

Sift 225g icing sugar into a bowl, add an egg white and 4 drops of essence of lavender and just enough violet-blue food colouring to create a shade of the lightest violet. Mix to a good paste and set aside for 10 minutes to rest. Tip onto an icing sugar-dusted surface and roll out to about 1cm in thickness. Use the smallest biscuit shapers to cut out. Dry out on baking parchment.

Twelfth Night Cake

I like to make a Twelfth Night Cake, a lemon sponge filled with raspberry fool and iced with a layer of marzipan and pale blue rolled icing scattered with yellow or golden stars. Eaten as dessert with a glass of wassail or my mulled white wine, it sort of marks an end to the festive period, an end to the old year and a start on the new.

Candied orange dipped in chocolate

Melt 250g good dark chocolate in a heatproof bowl over a saucepan of simmering water. Once the chocolate is completely melted add $\frac{1}{2}$ teaspoon golden syrup or runny honey - this will make the chocolate nice and glossy. Slice candied orange peel into 50mm wide strips and dip into the chocolate. Place on a cake rack to harden and serve with coffee.

Makes 18 biscuits

225g plain flour
½ teaspoon mixed spice
1 teaspoon ground ginger
1 teaspoon ground cinnamon
½ teaspoon salt
½ teaspoon bicarbonate of soda
100g butter
75g soft brown sugar
3 tablespoons golden syrup

Icing
1 egg white
1 teaspoon lemon juice
500g icing sugar, sifted

Gingerbread Biscuits

In medieval Europe spicy ginger biscuits made with almonds, flour or breadcrumbs, sweetened with honey and gilded with egg yolk and saffron or gold leaf were served as sweetmeats or given as favours. Fill your home with the fragrance of baking gingerbread and seasonal cheer. This recipe is simple; stir up the dough and enjoy rolling and shaping. Decorate the cooked biscuits with white icing or gild with edible gold leaf, then wrap as gifts or thread with ribbon to decorate the Christmas tree.

1 Preheat the oven to 170°C/325°F/gas mark 3. Lightly butter a baking tray or line with baking parchment.

2 Sieve the flour, spices, salt and bicarbonate of soda into a large bowl. Use a metal spoon to mix lightly. Place the butter, sugar and syrup in a medium saucepan and melt over a low heat, stirring occasionally.

3 Make a well in the centre of the dry ingredients and pour in the melted butter and sugar mixture and mix together. When the mixture has formed a ball, turn it out onto a clean dry surface and roll out to a thickness of 3mm.

4 Dip biscuit cutters lightly into flour and cut out shapes. Place on the baking tray. If you wish to thread the finished biscuits with ribbon, use a drinking straw to cut a hole in each shape.

5 Bake for 10–12 minutes until golden brown, then remove from the oven and place biscuits on a wire rack to cool.

6 To make the icing, whip the egg white lightly, add the lemon juice and stir. Add the icing sugar a spoonful at a time until you have a good consistency. Use a piping bag and a writing nozzle to decorate the biscuits.

Christmas Biscuits

Makes 18 biscuits

100g softened butter
100g caster sugar
1 small egg
1 teaspoon vanilla extract
200g plain flour, sifted
½ teaspoon baking powder

Preheat the oven to 180°C/350°F/gas mark 4. Cream the butter and sugar, add the egg and vanilla extract then use a spatula to mix in the sifted flour and baking powder. You may need to add a teaspoon or so of water to bring the mixture to a soft dough. Shape into a thick rectangle then place on a covered plate and refrigerate for half an hour. Roll out on a floured surface and cut out festive shapes, place on a baking tray, paint with a little water then sprinkle with granulated sugar, refrigerate for 15 minutes then bake for about 15 minutes, or until cooked. Try not to let them brown.

winter

Stollen Bread

Slices of stollen eaten freshly baked and sliced with mugs of hot chocolate are a seasonal pleasure.

Makes 1 large or 2 small loaves

100g sultanas
100g raisins
50g chopped mixed peel
4 tablespoons brandy
10g dried yeast
1 teaspoon sugar
50ml warm milk
60ml warm water
225g bread flour
½ teaspoon salt
25g sugar
1½ teaspoons mixed spice
1½ teaspoons ground cinnamon
125g softened butter
1 egg
25g butter and a little icing
   sugar, to finish

Marzipan
75g ground almonds
40g caster sugar
25g icing sugar
1 egg

1   Soak the dried fruit and peel in the brandy for 2 hours. Place the yeast, sugar, milk and water in a small warmed bowl and whisk. Set aside until frothy (about 30 minutes).

2   Sift the flour and salt into a large mixing bowl, add the sugar and spices and toss to mix. Rub in the butter.

3   Whisk the egg into the yeast mixture and pour into the dry ingredients. Use a spatula or spurtle to mix to a good dough. Oil your hands with a little olive oil or butter and knead for 5 minutes; the dough will be sticky, so do not add more flour. Return the dough to the bowl, cover with a clean tea towel and set in a warm, draught-free corner to rise.

4   Now make the marzipan (of course, you could buy a block of marzipan!). Place the ground almonds and sugars in a bowl. Break the egg into a small bowl and whisk, then add a tablespoon of egg to the dry mixture and stir well, bringing together a good firm marzipan dough. You may need to add a little more egg but do not overdo it. Reserve a small amount of the whisked egg.

5   Punch down the risen stollen dough and turn out onto an oiled surface. Pat into a wide rectangle. Take the prepared marzipan and roll into a rectangle. Place the rolled marzipan on the stollen dough and roll the whole up like a Swiss roll. Brush a little of the remaining whisked egg along the edge and press together.

6   Set on a buttered and floured baking tray and brush with more whisked egg. Put in a warm place to rise for 30 minutes.

7   Preheat the oven to 220°C/425°F/gas mark 7, then bake the bread for 35 minutes or until golden brown.

8   Remove from the oven, brush with 25g melted butter and dust with icing sugar. Eat warm or cold or toasted.

Magical Mince Pies

My Christmas begins when I check my dried fruit supplies and write a list: I will need to make fruit mince for the pies, and a couple of spare jars to give away as gifts, then there is the Christmas pudding to be stirred up on a Saturday afternoon when everyone is at home so each can make their wish for the coming year. Finally the Christmas cake, with a few individual Christmas cakes, to be marzipaned and iced as gifts.

Fruit Mince

Makes about 4 jars

250g raisins

250g currants

125g mixed peel

125g dried cherries

125g dried cranberries

125g sultanas

250g vegetable suet

3 tablespoons brandy

2 medium cooking apples

juice and zest of 1 orange

Chop the apples into tiny cubes and tip into a large bowl. Add all the remaining ingredients and mix well together. Store in jars.

Pastry

500g plain flour

250g butter

2 tablespoon iced water

50g caster sugar

Preheat the oven to 180°C/350°F/gas mark 4. Sift the flour into a large mixing bowl, add the butter and use your fingertips to rub in. Add a little iced water to bring to a soft but firm dough. Refrigerate for 30 minutes. Butter a mince pie tray. Roll out the pastry and use a biscuit cutter or the rim of a glass to shape the right sized circles of pastry. Cut a second set of small circles to cover the little pies with. If I find I am running out of pastry I sometimes cut a little star shape out of the lids. I then cover some pies with a pastry lid and others with just a sugar topped pastry star. Bake for 15 minutes.

Florentines

Makes 30

100g softened butter

6 tablespoons single cream

150g caster sugar

100g roughly chopped almonds

150g candied peel

50g chopped walnuts

200g glace cherries

6 tablespoons plain flour

Preheat the oven to 180°C/350°F/gas mark 4. Place the butter, cream and sugar in a large saucepan over a low heat until melted. Remove from the heat and fold in the remaining ingredients. Place spoonfuls on a buttered baking tray and bake for 8 minutes. Once baked, remove from the tray and cool on a cake rack. Packed into pretty boxes these make lovely Christmas favours.

WINTER REMEDIES

Cider vinegar, rosemary, sage - our grandmothers used these and much more to create hair rinses, cold cures, tonics and conditioners. I often rinse my hair in a weak solution of cider vinegar – it really works.

And so to bed...

If you have difficulty sleeping, grate a little nutmeg onto a cup of hot milk and drink just before bedtime. I swear by it.

Mustard plaster

Mix a tablespoon of mustard powder with half a cup of flour and water to make a thick paste. Spread across a double layer of muslin and cover with a second layer. Lay this across your chest for no more than 10 minutes at a time to treat a chesty cough.

Cider and rosemary cure

If you feel a cold coming on, boil a large sprig of rosemary in some cider for 5 minutes. Strain into a glass and carry up to bed, get under the covers and drink. This cure is said to induce sweating which will kill the cold.

Vinegar and brown paper

This isn't just a nursery rhyme. Soak a folded sheet of brown paper in a half and half solution of cider vinegar and water and lay across your forehead. The fumes are said to relieve headaches caused by falls, as well as being a good hangover remedy.

Caring for your crowning glory

My grandmother once told me how, when they were girls on the farm, they would set out bowls and buckets to save rainwater to wash their hair. The family lived in the Little Karroo, water came from either the well or the river and in those days before commercial hair products wise women would use a good hair brush and rainwater, vinegar rinses, herbs and oils to keep their crowning glory lustrous lookin'.

My grandmother had a good head of thick dark hair, which she washed weekly – the final rinse always a jug of cool rainwater with a little added cider vinegar, which in her words 'settled her hair'. Every evening she would brush her hair 50 strokes, moving the natural oils right to the tips, and occasionally she would twirl lengths of hair snipping off split ends with sharp scissors.

Sage Hair Tonic

If used regularly this tonic is said to restore natural colour to greying hair.

Place 2 tablespoons dried sage in a jam jar of water, place in a saucepan of water and boil for 2 hours, then strain the liquid, return it to the jar and every day comb some of the liquid through your hair. Store in the fridge for up to 10 days.

Coconut Oil Conditioner

Place a bottle of coconut oil in boiling water to liquidise. Comb the oil through your hair, about half a cupful should be enough. Wrap your hair with a towel kept specifically for the purpose. Leave for a couple of hours then wash out and condition.

Olive Oil Conditioner

Massage half a cup of olive oil into your scalp and comb through your hair. Leave for an hour before washing and conditioning as usual.

Cider Vinegar Conditioner

Add about a quarter of a cup of cider vinegar to a jug of cool water for the final rinse after washing your hair.

Herbal rinses

To bring out lustre, rinse fair hair in chamomile tea and dark hair in sage tea. If you would like a few summer highlights, rinse your hair in a mild lemon juice solution and dry in the sun.

winter

163

Sprouting beans

You will need a jam jar, a handkerchief-sized square of muslin or net, an elastic band, seeds to sprout and clean water.

Wash out the jam jar, place a tablespoon of seeds into the jar, and cover with clean water. Cover the jar with a square of muslin or net held in place with an elastic band. Leave to soak for an hour or so. Drain off the water. Set the jar aside, away from sunlight, to allow nature to do its work.

Over the next few days rinse the seeds in clean water twice a day. You should notice the seeds beginning to sprout. Once they have achieved a sufficient size, use them in salads or stir fries.

Seeds to sprout

Chickpeas, mustard and cress, lentils, alfalfa, soya beans, flax, coriander, sunflower

HEALTHY EATING

I have always been of the opinion that a healthy diet includes plain live yogurt and plenty of salads, in other words raw foods should be eaten every day. Winter salads can be just as interesting as summer salads – try them dressed with a little olive oil and a blob of yogurt instead of mayonnaise.

Coleslaw

Slice half a small white cabbage as thinly as you can and chop roughly so no slice is longer than 4cm. Place in a bowl along with 3 large carrots and 3 apples, both grated, and a finely chopped onion. I add about half a cup of raisins. To make the dressing spoon 4 heaped tablespoons mayonnaise into a small bowl. Add 5 tablespoons olive oil and 3 tablespoons vinegar. Whisk to mix then toss into the prepared vegetables and you have coleslaw.

Carrot, mustard and cress

1kg carrots, grated
mustard and cress sprouts
2 tablespoons mustard seeds

Dressing
4 tablespoons olive oil
1 tablespoon cider vinegar
½ teaspoon salt
sprinkling of black pepper
1 teaspoon caster sugar

Mix all the dressing ingredients together. Place the grated carrots and mustard and cress sprouts in a bowl, add the mustard seeds and dressing, toss all together and serve.

Home-made Yogurt

My mother used to have a yogurt plant (kefir), given to her by a Middle Eastern friend – a white cauliflower-like fungus of some sort that was put in warmed milk and left overnight. The next morning there would be yogurt. The yogurt would be poured through a colander and the white bits removed to be washed through with cold running water before being added to the next pint of warm milk. There was always plenty of yogurt to eat with fruit or a blob of jam or drink whisked up with iced water.

Makes 500ml yogurt
500ml whole milk
4 tablespoons live yogurt

Bring the milk almost to the boil, pour into a clean jug, cover and allow to cool until comfortably warm. Whisk in the yogurt then cover with a doily or clean piece of muslin, and top with a tea cosy. Set aside for 4–6 hours, by which time the milk should have turned into yogurt.

MARMALADE

Graham Short is one of my dearest friends, I've known him since I was a young girl and he was already old, so long in fact that he has become an integral part of my life. He makes the best marmalade I've ever tasted, deliciously tangy, perfectly chunky it is pure gold.

Seville Orange Marmalade

Makes 2 jars

600g Seville oranges
1 litre water
sugar
juice of 1 lemon

Cut the oranges in half and squeeze out the juice. Set aside.

Simmer the orange peel and pips with the water in a saucepan until the pith easily comes away from the peel. This should take about an hour of gently simmering. Allow to cool.

Using very clean hands and dealing with half an orange at a time, lift from the water, squeeze well, use a spoon to scrape away as much pith as will easily come away and place the treated orange in a clean bowl. Work your way through the fruit.

Now drain the liquor and orange remnants through a muslin-lined colander into a bowl. Gather the corners of the muslin together and squeeze well, collecting any remaining liquid in the bowl.

Next, use a sharp knife and a cutting board to shred the peel. (I prefer fairly chunky slices; you may prefer fine slices.) Add the shredded peel to the liquor. Add the saved orange juice. Now, using a cup or mug, measure into the cooking pot, counting cupfuls as you go. You will need to add a cup of sugar for each cup of orange mixture.

Squeeze a lemon and add the juice to the pot and place a saucer in the freezer section of your fridge.

Place the pot on the stove and bring slowly to the boil, stirring constantly with a wooden spoon to ensure the sugar melts and nothing sticks. Once boiling, remove the spoon and observe. At first the mixture will bubble up, frothy and slowly. As the minutes pass the bubbles will take on a new rhythm, bubbling merrily. The bubbling will then slow down to a measured beat. This should take about 12–15 minutes.

Now it is time to check for set. Remove the saucer from the freezer. Take a clean spoon and place a blob of marmalade on the saucer, wait a few moments, then check to see if a skin is forming across the surface of the blob. If so your marmalade is ready to pot; if not, continue boiling for 4 or 5 minutes then try again.

Once your marmalade has a skin, set has been achieved. Remove the pot from the heat. Wait a couple of minutes to allow it to go off the boil then use a ladle to pour into clean prepared jars. Cover and set aside to cool. Label and store.

Preparing jars for preserving

Wash jars well and remove any remnants of jam etc. Soak in hot water and bicarbonate of soda to remove labels. Wash lids in the same way.

Fill jam pots with boiling water just prior to bottling, pour the boiling water away and immediately filling the pots with jam, cover with a greaseproof disc and screw the lid on tight.

If you prefer, you may want to sterilise clean prepared jars. To do this place jars in a roasting dish and warm to a temperature of 140°C/275°F/Gas mark 1 in the oven – keep at this temperature for 10 minutes. Remove and immediately fill with preserve, cover and seal.

STEAMED PUDDINGS

A good steamed pudding results from simple ingredients, carefully weighed and measured, creamed and stirred together and simmered in a pudding basin for what sometimes seems like hours and hours. Presented, turned out and steaming on a plate, dripping with sauce or syrup, a steamed pudding can bring the perfect meal to a delicious conclusion.

Blood Orange Sauce

juice and rind of 2 blood oranges
2 tablespoons unbleached white sugar
150ml water

Use a lemon rind peeler to strip curls of rind from the blood oranges. Squeeze out their juice and strain away the pips. Bring the water and orange rind to the boil, then simmer for 5 minutes. Allow to cool. Add the sugar and orange juice, stirring constantly, bring to the boil and simmer for 5 minutes.

Cranberry and Blood Orange Pudding

Serves 4

175g softened butter
175g unbleached white sugar
3 eggs
175g self-raising flour
1 tablespoon lemon juice
juice of half an orange
60g dried cranberries
1.2 litre pudding basin
greaseproof paper and string or a pudding cloth

1 Butter the pudding basin and sprinkle lightly with flour, shake out any excess flour. Set aside. Cream the butter and sugar, add the eggs and a little flour, continue mixing, add lemon juice, orange juice, then fold in the remaining flour, mixing well. Finally fold in the cranberries. Spoon the mixture into the pudding basin, cover and tie with pleated greaseproof paper.

2 Place the basin on an upturned saucer in a large saucepan containing boiling water; the water should come halfway up the sides of the basin. Cover and bring to the boil, then leave to simmer for 2½ hours. Top up water levels as needed.

3 Once cooked, lift the pudding bowl from the saucepan, remove the paper and gently run the tip of a knife around the edge of the pudding before inverting onto a warmed serving plate.

Pudding cloths

Nowadays we use pudding bowls with lids or greaseproof paper folded and tied to keep puddings in check as they sit simmering away in a saucepan. My grandmother used a pudding cloth, rinsed in boiling water, well rung out and thoroughly floured. Flour side down the cloth would be laid over the bowl, secured with string, with the four corners tied together to enable safe retrieval from the pot.

Washing pudding cloths

Soak used pudding cloths in a saucepan of cold water to which a little bicarb has been added, set aside for an hour or two then place over the heat and bring slowly to the boil. Allow to boil for a few minutes then rinse well in cold water and hang out to dry.

Sticky Toffee Pudding

Serves 4

100g fresh dates
100ml water
½ teaspoon bicarbonate of soda
100g unsalted softened butter
100g unbleached sugar
2 eggs
100g self-raising flour
½ teaspoon vanilla extract
1.2 litre pudding basin
greaseproof paper and string or a pudding cloth

Toffee sauce
100g unsalted butter
100g light brown sugar
100ml double cream

1 Butter the pudding basin and sprinkle lightly with flour, shake out any excess flour. Set aside.

2 Remove the stones and any stalk ends from the dates. Place dates, water and bicarb in a small saucepan and bring to a gentle simmer, cook for 5 minutes, then remove from the heat and mash with a potato masher or blend lightly. Leave to cool. In the meantime, cream the butter and sugar, when light and fluffy add the eggs, flour and vanilla extract, mix, then fold in the cooled date mixture.

3 Spoon the mixture into the pudding basin. Cover and tie with greaseproof paper or a pudding cloth. Steam for 2 hours.

4 To make the sauce, simply place all the ingredients in a saucepan and heat slowly, keeping an eye on it to make sure it doesn't burn. Bring to the boil and allow to bubble for a minute or two then remove from the heat and the sauce is ready to pour over the cooked pudding.

Steamed Syrup Pudding

Serves 4

175g softened butter
175g unbleached white sugar
grated rind and juice of half a lemon
3 eggs
4 tablespoons golden syrup
1.2 litre pudding basin
greaseproof paper and string or a pudding cloth

Butter the pudding basin and sprinkle lightly with flour, shake out any excess flour. Set aside.

In a large mixing bowl place the softened butter, sugar and lemon juice and rind, and cream until the mixture is light and fluffy. Add the eggs, one at a time, alternating with small spoonfuls of flour. Fold in remaining flour.

Slowly pour about 4 tablespoons of syrup into the bottom of the prepared pudding basin. Add the pudding mix to the basin, taking care not to scrape at the buttered and floured bowl. Cover with pleated greaseproof paper or a pudding cloth.

Follow steps 3, 4 and 5 on p.168. I always pour a little more syrup over the pudding and serve it immediately with plenty of Real Custard (*see p.31*).

Whisky Marmalade Pudding

Serves 4

175g softened butter
175g unbleached white sugar
grated rind and juice of half a lemon
3 eggs
4 tablespoons marmalade
2 tablespoons whisky
1.2 litre pudding basin
greaseproof paper and string or a pudding cloth

Butter the pudding basin and sprinkle lightly with flour, shake out any excess flour. Set aside.

In a large mixing bowl place the softened butter, sugar and lemon juice and rind, and cream until the mixture is light and fluffy. Add the eggs, one at a time alternating with small spoonfuls of flour. Fold in the remaining flour, marmalade and whisky.

Spoon the pudding mix into the basin, taking care not to scrape at the buttered and floured sides. Cover with pleated greaseproof paper or a pudding cloth and tie with string.

Follow steps 3, 4 and 5 on p.168. Sometimes I make a little sauce by melting a few tablespoons of marmalade along with a couple of whisky and pour that over the pudding before it is presented at the table. Serve with Real Custard (*see p.31*).

Index

index

Useful addresses

The internet is a very useful resource for ordering materials. The following email order companies supply around the world.

Flavourings and essences, natural cosmetic and cleaning ingredients:

THE SOAP KITCHEN
Units 2 D&E Hatchmoor Ind/Est
Torrington, EX38 7HP
United Kingdom
www.thesoapkitchen.co.uk
richard@thesoapkitchen.co.uk
Tel: +44 (0)1805 622944
Fax: +44 (0)870 4586724

Space Dust Retro Sweeties
http://www.britishcandy.com

Edible gold leaf
http://www.feuillesdor.com/en/index-en.htm